RETURN ON PRINCIPLE

RETURN ON PRINCIPLE

7 Core Values to Help Protect Your Money in Good Times and Bad

■

DAVID J. SCRANTON
CLU, ChFC, CFP®, CFA, MSFS

ADVISORS' ACADEMY
PRESS

RETURN ON PRINCIPLE

Published by
ADVISORS' ACADEMY PRESS
Pompano Beach, Florida

ISBN 978-0-9975441-0-7
Ebook ISBN 978-0-9975441-1-4

FIRST EDITION

Book Design by Neuwirth & Associates
Jacket Design by Neuwirth & Associates.

Manufactured in the United States of America

10 9 8 7 6 5 4 3 2

To Mom, who made me what I am today.

CONTENTS

RETURN ON PRINCIPLE

INTRODUCTION

THIS ISN'T JUST a book about investing. There are plenty of those. If you go to Amazon and search for the word "investing," you'll find more than 83,000 books. Most will tell you what you want to hear. What you expect to hear.

In nearly every case, you'd be better off saving the time and money you'd waste on those books. This book is different. It has to be. Because I'm different. I don't do what Wall Street tells me to do. I can't stand the stress of watching my clients' money drop 50 percent or more in a downturn. I despise waiting years just to see it come back around to breakeven, like that's something to celebrate.

This book is about investing in a safer way than anyone has likely ever taught you. It's a book about learning how to zig when the entire world around you is telling you to zag. And it's about building your life on the right principles because you know you've protected yourself from market storms and built a storm cellar for a better future.

Sure, those other books will tell you to "buy low, sell high." If you live in America in the twenty-first century and haven't heard that before, I'd be surprised. Of course, those other books also tell you to stay in the market no matter what happens. Why shouldn't they? It's not *their* money. The investment companies that write books get paid if you invest with them—whether your stocks or mutual funds go up or down. They can watch your life savings go from $2 million to $1 million in a year and they'll sound sympathetic. They might even *be* sympathetic. But they also got paid every step along the way from $2 million to $1 million. Just as they know they'll get paid if you leave the money with them and watch it try to claw back to breakeven. Las Vegas gamblers tell you never to gamble what you can't afford to lose. Yet nearly half of all Americans do that when they drop their savings, their retirement, and their kids' college fund into the stock market.

Years ago, I decided there had to be a better way—before I watched the dot-com implosion tear apart the markets in 2000. Then I watched the worst economic downturn since the Great Depression, spawned by the 2007–2009 market collapse. I helped my clients avoid those disasters, but that's still not enough. I spent years working up ways to help you invest for the long haul without putting your entire life on a roulette table and watching a stranger spin the wheel. That's what this book is about: helping you discover that there is a safer way to invest, and teaching you more about the markets—solid principles to build your future on. You might just discover that much of what you think you know is just not true.

In the movie *The Matrix*, Laurence Fishburne's character, Morpheus, tried to teach Neo (played by Keanu Reeves) that their world wasn't what it seemed. "You take the blue pill, the story ends, you wake up in your bed and believe whatever you want to believe," he told Neo. "You take the red pill, you stay in Wonderland, and I show you how deep the rabbit hole goes."

I'm asking you to take the red pill. Not to learn a mighty conspiracy or launch into a hatred of Wall Street. I don't want that. I simply want you to learn what Wall Street doesn't want you to know—that there's a better way.

Some Basic Definitions for You

I promise not to get too technical, but there are a couple of definitions you are going to need to get started: A bull market exists when the stock market is generally trending upward in value and a bear market exists when the stock market is doing poorly. Both bear markets and bull markets can be either cyclic or secular in nature. A cyclic cycle is shorter term and a secular cycle is longer term. As you read on, you will learn that the 2008 market crash was actually a cyclic bear market inside of a secular bear market.

So the question then becomes, what exactly do we mean when we say "stock market"? In general, the term *stock market* embraces all stocks that are being traded through the New York Stock Exchange, the NASDAQ, and any other such exchanges. For purposes of this book, though, when we use the term *stock market*, we're going to be referring primarily to an index. An index is a hypothetical compilation of a certain number of stocks. It is technically not possible to invest in an index, but there are mutual funds and exchange traded funds that do a pretty good job at copying the holdings in the index.

The most common index is the Dow Jones Industrial Average (DJIA). However, we are going to use the Standard & Poor's 500 index in this book whenever possible. The reason is that the DJIA includes only 30 stocks whereas the S&P 500 includes 500 stocks.

Therefore, the S&P 500 is a better overall indicator of the stock market. Also, the S&P 500 is calculated in a way that does not allow the bigger companies, with higher market capitalization, to overly affect the index. Not only is it a broader index at 500 stocks, but it is also calculated more fairly and is, we believe, a better representation of the overall market.

However, there are some times in this book where we have to refer to the Dow. The Standard & Poor's 500 started in 1926, which is why a lot of market data begins in 1926. But the S&P 500 index was very small until 1957, when it expanded to include 500 stocks. I generally consider 1957 to be the beginning of the S&P 500 index. The Dow Jones Industrial Average started in 1896. So again, we use the S&P 500 as a proxy for the market whenever we can, but in some cases, we have to revert to the Dow.

Okay, now you are through the hard part; the rest of the book should be a piece of cake!

1

FINANCIAL OVERPROTECTION

W HEN DISASTER STRIKES, it demands everything we have to think about something else. Once it's over, it takes incredible will to recall what happened so that we can try to understand it. That's the follow-up story of the 2007–2009 market crash: understanding what happened.

On October 9, 2007, the Standard & Poor's 500 closed at 1,565.15—a gain of more than 50 percent since July 23, 2002.[1] The bulls were out in force and market insanity had momentum. Investment houses, mutual fund companies, advisors, and ordinary investors had only one thing on their minds.

Buy.

Buy and keep on buying. Grab your money sitting in a certificate of deposit (CD) and invest it in the stock market. Get in and get rich. For advisors who worked in the field, the call volume was

---

1 "^GSPC Historical Prices," *Yahoo! Finance*, 2009, https://finance.yahoo.com/q/hp?s=%5EG SPC&a=08&b=1&c=2001&d=07&e=30&f=2002&g=d

enormous. Investors all wanted in. You could see the energy, the excitement on TV. If you were in an airport and the TV showed the closing bell, everyone would turn and watch.

The bell would clang at 4 p.m. and the guests on the podium would all smile and shake one another's hand, as if they had been part of something momentous. They were personally keeping the great engine of Wall Street running, just like they were in the driver's seat of a Lamborghini going up a hill. And up. And up.

Investors watched all around the world, but especially in the United States. With each clang of that bell, they'd contemplate their own investments.

And celebrate!

The Dow was up another 50 or 100 points. People would open their monthly investment statements and cheer. Their stocks and mutual funds were kicking butt. Everyone who invested felt smart. America was on the right track.

The financial world was filled to the brim with excitement. It had the aura of a hometown team during the World Series. Wall Street was back, and the dot-com disaster was an afterthought.

Who could blame them? Success is self-reinforcing. The more you succeed, the smarter you feel and the more you strive to succeed even more. A cyclical bull market had taught Americans that they were destined once more to be rich.

A few of us weren't comfortable with market madness. I'll be honest; I was downright worried. I'm careful with my own money. I try to be overly careful and overly protective with the money my clients entrust to me. It just wouldn't be right to do otherwise.

In my October 2007 newsletter, I said investors should be careful and not allow themselves to be "lured into a false sense of security." Instead of urging my clients to plow more money into stocks, I was reminding them of the 2000–2003 stock market drop and warning them that we could be about to begin another drop, possibly of greater magnitude than the last.

I didn't realize it at the time, but the market peaked on October 9, 2007. That October high soon turned into a slide that took a few percentage points off the top. More drops followed, and investors began to worry. That fear gripped people as they turned on the TV, so many left it turned off. Monthly investment statements went unopened. It wasn't really bad news if you didn't admit it.

By June 2008, the dreaded Wall Street bear had beaten the stuffing out of the bull. Investors were scared now. The market had shot right past correction territory and kept on falling. The following month, *BusinessWeek* told the world "How Wall Street Ate the Economy . . . and What Happens Now." Only the decline wasn't even close to being over.

With each month, things seemed to get worse. The economic tragedy of the American markets became global. Things got so bad that the economy became a political issue—both on the campaign trail and in the halls of Congress.

Fear had gripped the financial world. Washington turned to what became a trillion-dollar stimulus bill to keep the whole economy from cratering.

When the market had finally stopped falling, it was 2009. My estimate of 40 percent loss was actually a bit low. Turned out it was 53.78 percent. Many investors will never earn back what they lost.

I'm determined to help stop that from happening to you.

How I Learned to Value Overprotection

I have a degree in mathematics, and I have enough credentials as a financial planner that I can put seventeen letters after my name— CLU, ChFC, CFA, CFP®, and MSFS. But the best mentor I ever had never even finished high school. She could only put three letters after her name, though they were the best three: MOM.

My mother, Irene, instilled in me the most important skills anyone needs to handle other people's money: being very protective and detail-oriented. At the same time, this unbelievable woman taught me that I could be anything and anybody I wanted to be. And she did it all on her own.

She had to. My father died when I was almost four years old. It was called an "occupational accident." He went to work on construction one day and I never saw him again. He said to my mom, "OK, honey, I'll see you when I get home," and was out the door.

Mom got the horrible call about the accident in the middle of the day, saying they rushed him to the hospital and it didn't look good. A neighbor came over and took care of me while Mom went to the hospital. He was pronounced dead and—just like that—she was a single mother in an era when that was even tougher than it is today.

We had just moved to Massachusetts ten months earlier so Dad could take this job. After he died, rather than stay in the strange place, she sold the house and we went back to Connecticut to rebuild our lives.

She received a settlement of $50,000, which wasn't much but it gave us enough to get by. There weren't a lot of discussions of safety nets back then. Men and women took care of their own loved ones. People like my mom had few resources because they didn't have family money to fall back on. She learned to make do. Although my dad had been a traditional husband and father, Mom wasn't about to crumble under the weight of what happened. She was too strong for that. It just wasn't her nature. She had me to look out for.

Her hard-driving personality came naturally. It was who she was. Mom loved cars and loved driving them fast all her life. One of her nicknames from her younger days was "Hell on Wheels." She used to visit my dad, Eugene, sometimes when they were dating. He was still living with his parents, and Mom's future mother-in-law wasn't always happy about her driving habits. His parents would go to bed and my mom would kiss Eugene good-bye and get in her car and leave. Sometimes she'd accelerate a little too fast and spin her wheels.

My grandmother would come running out of her bedroom and yell, "Gene, will you tell that girlfriend of yours not to burn rubber when she leaves?" I'm guessing that was one of the many things my dad liked about my mom: her independence.

Mom would drive fast, but she was never careless—either with her driving or when it came to her son. She was the opposite. She had lost my father and she wasn't going to lose me. She wasn't someone who let fear rule her. But she would worry that I'd get hit by a car or be in some kind of an accident. Who could blame her? She and I only had each other. These days, I think we better appreciate how difficult that situation can be. She had to be both mom and dad and raise a boy to grow into a man.

I was damn lucky to have her.

On the surface, some would argue that my mom wasn't really prepared to raise a son on her own. She came from a poor, working-class family and dropped out of high school to work and help pay the bills. It wasn't exactly a nurturing environment. She must have learned what not to do, because somehow she managed to put together a skill set to bring me up in a positive way.

There are thousands of ways that parents influence us. The good ways help us get started in life, and she was a natural. One of the most important things she'd do was just talk to me. Decades later, I still remember how she would sit on that little twin bed I had when I was six, seven, eight, and nine. Instead of reading to me, like lots of other parents, she'd sit on the foot of that bed and talk with me. At an age when my friends were hearing children's stories, my mom would talk to me and tell me about growing up.

The stories were inspirational but had a simple message. You could be anything you want in life. You could be a doctor, a lawyer, an astronaut. We didn't have much, but Mom told me that I could even be rich if that's what I wanted.

I've given my share of inspirational speeches. They can really motivate adults. But few parents give them to children. They lecture, cajole, harass, and yell. My mom chose to talk to me. It was unbelievably powerful. She had strength, a belief, and she passed it on to me every night. And those talks impact my life even today.

Her regular job was the same as most parents'—keeping her son out of trouble and teaching me as much as she could about how to be not just a man but a good one. She set down firm rules of where I could go, and I learned quickly that she was too sharp to let things slip by her.

She was devoted. Mom definitely had a knack for getting me to think she was watching me at all times. I remember a lesson I got one time in the first grade. My mother decided to check on me at recess. She parked near the school just before the students were let out. All of us kids came running out for recess, and I ran and tackled some boy. We were going to fight, though God only knows why. I was six or seven. I don't think I needed a reason.

Mom had a front-row seat to the fight.

It was more than enough for her. She pulled her car alongside us and slammed on the brakes. She got out, grabbed me by the arm, and pulled me off the other boy. So then, for the rest of my school career, every time I'd go to recess I'd be scanning the entire horizon, looking for her. I was convinced she was there.

Although financial overprotection is a very good thing, as a child, I didn't always appreciate Mom's overprotective nature. When all the kids were playing baseball, I could never go over to someone else's yard and play unless I could see or be seen from the house. Right up to age 12 or so, if I wanted to ride my bike, I could ride it down the street, but no further.

Another Milestone with Mom

I had been working out with weights at home and maxed out what I could do there. Mom told me to sign up for a gym. I was surprised and excited. I was able to have a place where I could hang out with the guys and be cool. She would drop me off and pick me up at the gym from about the time I was fourteen years old till I was sixteen, when I first started to drive.

The gym was an important opportunity for me. I'd been dabbling in weights and working out since I was a kid. Only now I wasn't just hanging around with my mom, at school, or even with friends my age. I was hanging out in a man's world.

The guys at the gym would call each other "big," as a sign of respect. I mean, if you work out, the whole goal is to get big. Calling you that meant it was working. It meant even more to me, a teenager. "Hey, here's Big Dave." "Look, it's Big Dave." It made me feel like an adult. I wasn't just a teen. I was one of the guys.

That was the way we all talked to each other. We would lift hundreds of pounds and talk tough. It was the land of testosterone. For a guy who hardly had a dad, it was an environment that let me feel macho.

My mother didn't care about all that. She hated waiting and if she came to pick me up from the gym and I wasn't standing by the door ready at 4:30, she'd make me pay by yelling across the gym in front of all the guys. She'd say, "Dave, get your butt over here. I'm not going to stand here and wait for you. I'm leaving."

She embarrassed me in front of all the guys, at first. But instead of undermining me, the guys accepted her and embraced her like she belonged. All of a sudden, they started calling her "Big Irene."

She was a slim lady, five feet seven and a half, and built small. But they called her "Big Irene" because all the guys in the gym were impressed by her. They knew she was no-nonsense. If she corrected somebody, they'd say, "Sorry, sorry, Mrs. Scranton."

They understood her better than almost anyone. All these years later and almost no one understood her as well as they did. They treated her with respect. They treated her like an equal. They knew she wasn't there to embarrass me. They knew she was there to look out for me. That was something these tough guys could relate to.

Even in a man's world like the gym, nobody messed with "Big Irene."

That sense of protection and sometimes even overprotection became a foundational principle for my life and my career. It helped make and save a lot of money for my clients, too.

It also altered the career path I was on in a huge way. It led me to find a new way of doing things. A way to protect my clients, especially with the looming storm in the markets.

How the Alphabet Soup after My Name Protected My Clients from Disaster

I started out in the insurance side of the business, but quickly got into the stock market. Through the 1990s I was using the stock market as a tool, just like every other advisor, to help my clients make money. Who wasn't? It was the tech boom. The Internet was still new and anything that ended in *dot-com* was going through the roof.

It was tech, tech, tech. Companies that made hardware and software were drawing investment and the trade publications were filled with new start-ups almost daily.

Everyone was going insane. I mean nuts with greed. You had barbers and cab drivers tuning into CNBC to watch their investments. All my clients wanted to be part of it. Commentators were talking as if the bulls were running down the streets of New York and the market would just keep shooting ever skyward if everyone just hopped onto a bull. I started getting a bad feeling in the pit of my stomach about it all.

It was bull all right, and it worried the hell out of me. "What goes up, must come down" rang in my head. While I was getting scared by the market, James Glassman and Kevin Hassett were hard at work publishing their book *Dow 36,000: The New Strategy for Profiting from the Coming Rise in the Stock Market.*

That book came out in October 1999. The DOW on October 1, 1999, was 10,273.[1] I got concerned about the stock market because I knew math and I knew history—a powerful combination if used correctly. In my studies of stock market history, I discovered there were certain consistently repeatable cycles going back and forth over the last 200 years. History didn't give me a term for what was going on in 1998 or 1999, except one that we all know well now: "bubble."

I didn't know what to do. As a Chartered Financial Analyst (CFA), my answer was that you go into the bond market. But there was a problem with that strategy. I was working as a broker then and it was hard to make a living selling a simple bond portfolio.

The market had me in a bind because it seemed apparent that things were about to turn sour. I didn't know what to do, but I knew I had to change my model. I had to do what I felt was right; I had to protect my clients.

This was the year before the tech bubble burst. By March 10, 2000, the NASDAQ, which housed many of the tech stocks, hit its all-time high of 5,048.62. Two and a half years later, on October 9, 2002, it had lost 77.93 percent of its value and was down to a measly 1,114.11.[2] If I had ignored my gut and looked after myself, I could have kept making big commissions on stocks and mutual funds that I believed weren't safe. I would have screwed all of my clients. I was once asked in an interview about the proudest moment of my career. It was really an easy answer: "I had the courage to change my business model when I realized my old model was no longer going to be in the best interest of my clients." And I did it in time to save my clients from the hell of the dot-com crash.

---

1   "Dow Jones Industrial Average," *Yahoo!Finance*, 2009, https://finance.yahoo.com/q/hp?s=%5EDJI&a=07&b=29&c=1999&d=10&e=30&f=1999&g=d

2   "NASDAQ Composite," *Yahoo!Finance*, 2009, http://finance.yahoo.com/q/hp?s=%5EIXIC&a=02&b=1&c=2000&d=09&e=15&f=2002&g=d

Sure, I like being right. Who wouldn't? And there's part of me that just likes zigging when everyone else zags, being a contrarian. But none of that matters when someone else's money is on the line. You have a moral and legal responsibility to do right by your client. It should never be about you. It's about protecting the client.

That crisis forced me to look at how I was doing things and revise my business model. I learned there are ways to potentially give a client peace of mind and solid profits in *any* market, and a retirement the client can count on without the terrifying risks of the market.

I've learned that many people don't want the headaches and the stress of having huge sums in a market that no one can predict consistently.

I've found what I believe to be a better solution.

That's why in 1999 I started telling my clients (and anyone else who would listen) there has to be a better way. Every time there's a crash, investors remember that growth can sometimes mean stocks shrink in value too.

Not everyone was receptive. I understand. Some people prefer shock and awe to a sane and rational approach to investing. But many people liked my idea. They liked being "overprotected." They grew tired of being troubled every morning, terrified by the gyrations in the markets. They wanted to know they'd built their financial life on a sound foundation, on solid principles.

Why not invest in ways that generate income? Why not use a strategy that gives you consistent dividends and interest you can count on? I think of it as investing the "old-fashioned way."

Others got caught up in the stock market, but some of those prospective clients came back to me after the tech bubble. The same thing happened during the market collapse of 2008; more people came back. They knew I had been right about trying to lower the risk. Now many of them are worried about a third drop, and they don't want to be stranded in the market when that happens.

I've built my business protecting hundreds of millions of dollars for clients who didn't want to lose it all, and I've succeeded.

A Strong Financial Defense

We don't have to live our financial lives fearing loss. The older you are and the closer to retirement you become, the more you want to avoid those big losses.

Let's envision a representative couple named Michelle and Tom. They've worked their whole lives and are both in their early sixties. Together, they've amassed $1 million in assets that they think will give them enough to live out a comfortable retirement when you factor in Social Security. That sounds good in theory. But it might not play out that way if they've got that nest egg in the stock market. Suppose the markets hit their third major drop. Even if it's not as bad as last time, the couple might be in trouble.

Let's say the S&P 500[1] index only slices 50 percent. Suddenly, Michelle and Tom are planning to retire with just $500,000. What happens to their quality of life? The last two downturns took 47.8 percent and 56.77 percent out of the market, respectively, so 50 percent is a pretty realistic number.

Recuperation Rate

If $1,000,000 gets reduced to $500,000 upon a 50 percent market decline, that means the remaining $500,000 has to double to get

---

1   "S&P 500," *Yahoo!Finance*, 2009, https://finance.yahoo.com/q/hp?s=%5EGSPC&a=00&b=2 &c=1998&d=00&e=22&f=2016&g=d&z=66&y=3894

Percentage of Loss	5%	10%	15%	20%	25%	30%	35%	40%	45%	50%	75%	90%
Gain to Break Even	5%	11%	18%	25%	33%	43%	54%	67%	82%	100%	300%	900%

(Figure 1—Recuperation Rate Table)

Source: Ken Faulkenberry, "Investment Risk Management Plan," http://www.arborinvest-
mentplanner.com/investment-risk-management-plan-value-investors/

back to a million dollars (see Figure 1). That represents a 100 percent gain and that's how the math works. All of that assumes that
Michelle and Tom kept their money in the markets. If they took out
money to pay bills, the recovery back to square one would take so
long it might end up being impossible.

If they are earning 5 percent per year on their remaining account
value, and they were smart enough to reduce their withdrawals,
their income now would amount to a mere $25,000 per year. Even
coupled with Social Security, that would be a major step down in
lifestyle for them. And even the reduced annual withdrawal rate
could render full recovery impossible. For example, if Tom and Michelle were invested in a simple S&P 500 index fund, by the end of
2013, they would only have $845,000 left in their nest egg (see Fig-
ure 2). Their withdrawals would have prevented full recovery even
though the stock market had finally surpassed January 2000 levels.

I wish this were the pessimistic view, but it's not. I used 50 percent as an example in my scenario.

Just remember our last market meltdown. The S&P dropped
56.77 percent from October 9, 2007, to March 9, 2009. You'd be left
with just 43.23 percent of your investments. Double that and you'd
still be underwater. That's right, a 100 percent gain wouldn't let
you break even. To get back even, your portfolio would have to go
straight up approximately 132 percent. That kind of success takes
time, and it depends on the market not dropping again.

S&P 500 by Month: October 2007 to March 2009

(Figure 2—S&P 500 by Month: October 2007 to March 2009)

Source: https://finance.yahoo.com/q/hp?s=%5EDJI&a=07&b=29&c=1999&d=10&e=30&f=1999&g=d

If the third drop happens, and if it merely equals the second one, Michelle and Tom will again have lost more than half of their assets. And so will almost half of all Americans.

Suppose this happened while they were actually planning to retire. They would have been left with an awful choice—sell into the market drop or try to ride it out and probably delay retirement for many years. Either way, they lose.

It's not quite as rough on younger investors because they have the time to recover from a fallen market. That still doesn't make it easy. From 2000 to 2013, even younger investors grew impatient with zero overall growth because of two major drops and recoveries during that time.

It takes a cast-iron constitution to handle that kind of uncertainty.

The Question to Ask about Risk

Many people are hardwired to be optimists. That's an admirable quality, but it has its drawbacks where investing is concerned. The main reason investors—even people who've been badly hurt by financial loses—continue to shortchange financial defense is that much of the financial services industry does likewise.

Unfortunately, a lot of people in the industry are salespeople first, advisors and educators second. Their first priority is to move product. Obviously, it's easier to push investments that are "sexier" and well known. That means stock-based products.

For salespeople, the stock market is the path of least resistance, the easiest sell. There's a whole industry based on promoting it. The daily news promotes it. Even Hollywood talks stocks in its movies and TV shows. (Coincidentally, the stock market also happens to be the one path with the best potential to earn advisors high fees and commissions over the long run. Hmmm.)

Logical people don't take risks like that "just because." They might go skydiving for the excitement. Few will toss their life savings out the window to see where it lands.

Imagine I was willing to box one of the champs—Muhammad Ali in his heyday, or Mike Tyson, or Wladimir Klitschko. I might live through a round and eventually I'd heal. But why bother? Why endure all of that pain for no gain?

Now, if someone offered me a purse of $10 million just for fighting, I'd at least have to consider it. Because there'd be enough of a prize in exchange for the risk. That's a more realistic risk/reward for something that insane.

We understand this. Look at the TV game show *Jeopardy*. When the three contestants get to Final Jeopardy, they are given a category and told to make a bet before they are given the question. Contestants have to weigh their own likelihood of winning, taking into account the scores of the other players and their own chance of knowing the answer.

> It hasn't worked that way in the financial world. Financial advisors and publications have taught us that it's only our "risk tolerance level" that determines how much risk we should take. They totally skip the other half of the question: How likely am I to get rewarded for taking all that stock market risk? Of course, asking that question would presuppose that you could foresee the upside or downside in advance.

Every single time, the contestants are trying to determine their chances of being rewarded for their risk. The financial world doesn't want us to think that way because it prefers that we believe the markets are totally random.

So ask yourself the question now: How likely are you to be rewarded by the current market? Is that reward worth putting your entire life savings on the line?

You should be having questions now. Because there are alternatives for you if you don't want to seek stock market growth—and risk shrinkage. There's also the option of investing for income instead of growth. Good, old-fashioned, boring, boring income in your pocket in the form of interest and dividends. Even if you don't need that income right away, you can reinvest and keep your money growing.

It's a strategy to remove the pain from your day-to-day life. I know, because that's what I did in my own financial universe. I decided that stock market insanity wasn't good for my financial, physical, or mental health. I just said, "No."

As a result, I'm in a good place if I wanted to retire today, and my finances aren't at as great a risk if the third drop happens. That strategy yields results that let me know I've built my financial house on what I consider a solid foundation, on the right principles.

Winning with Defense

The great Alabama football coach Paul "Bear" Bryant once said, "Defense wins championships," and you can bet that every great coach in every sport has tried that same Crimson Tide philosophy.

Just think about some of the great sports dynasties, teams that won championships year after year: the Green Bay Packers under Vince Lombardi, the Boston Celtics under Red Auerbach, and the Yankees under Joe Torre. You could go on and on.

All of these teams knew how to score, yes, but they all started with the premise that a strong defense made their offense better. Strategically, they knew how to win games. Still, they focused first on strategies that ensured they wouldn't lose.

That same approach is critical when it comes to your finances and, in particular, saving and investing for retirement. When you're talking about your "life savings," losses can potentially have a huge impact on your life!

Again, the fact of the matter is, this very thing has happened to domestic investors in the United States twice in the last fifteen years. Remember, from January 2000 through March 2003, the Standard & Poor's 500 stock index dropped nearly 50 percent and took until October 2007 to recover. It took approximately three years for the market to drop that much and then four and a half years to make a 100 percent gain and get back to where it was some seven and a half years earlier. Then it dropped again—this time, 56.77 percent—and again took roughly six years to recover to its previous high.

Let's say a man named Harry retired in 2000 and stayed invested in the stock market. To supplement his Social Security, he started to draw income from his investments. Assume his portfolio value was $1 million and he was taking out $50,000 per year.

He's expecting that sum would last him throughout his retirement—figuring twenty years of $50,000 plus whatever his stocks grew while he was retired.

Only he retired in 2000. And from 2000 to 2013 the market dropped by 50 percent and then recovered and then dropped again by almost 60 percent and then recovered. That's a net result of zero growth over fourteen years. Zero!

Let's say Harry wasn't as smart as our other investors, Tom and Michelle, because he continued to take out $50,000 a year over that time. He would have spent $700,000 out of his portfolio. With zero growth, simple math says that in 2013, he would have had $300,000 left.

Unfortunately, however, the impact would have been far worse. That's because in the years when the stock market dropped and Harry was still needing to take out his $50,000 per year, his investment advisor or mutual fund company had to liquidate more shares to give him that same amount of income. He did the reverse of buying low and selling high. He had to sell low after buying high.

As a result, Harry cannibalized the fund. By the time the market came back in 2013, he would only have had $285,000 remaining, including dividends. That is $560,000 less than Tom and Michelle and a fraction of Harry's original portfolio! His long-term outlook went from a comfortable retirement to a very uncomfortable one. In just fourteen years.

Two drops of approximately 50 percent and subsequent rebounds from 2000 to 2013. Are those the kind of founding principles on which you want to build your future? Of course not.

Time Is Money

Let's consider an important question: When the markets dropped, just how huge was the impact on investors oblivious to the importance of financial defense? And yes, they may still have been investing most of their remaining money in the market despite those two major drops. If they were too worried and paralyzed by events to make the necessary decisions (I think of it as a form of financial

PTSD—posttraumatic stress disorder), maybe the following information would have changed their minds.

First, there's the fact that these investors have twice had to redouble their lost gains. Meanwhile they experienced virtually no portfolio growth over that entire period of almost a decade and a half.

Then there's another factor. We also need to consider the amount of time that elapsed. For an investor to recover from a 50 percent loss with a 100 percent gain in a few years isn't easy. In that sense, investors from March 2003 to October 2007 were lucky; they made that 100 percent gain in only four and a half years. That represented an annual average growth rate of about 16 percent. Unfortunately, all those gains only helped them to break even. The same thing happened again when the market recovered after the financial crisis from 2009 through 2013. This time, the market more than doubled in four and a half years to regain its previous losses.

Even that sounds pretty good until you factor in a little thing called inflation. Over the last fifteen years, investors lost approximately 27 percent of their buying power due to inflation. What was worth a dollar fifteen years ago was by the end of last year worth only 73 cents.

Then we have to factor in a pesky little detail called "lost opportunity cost." Whether we're talking four, seven, or fourteen years, consider the fact that investors waiting and hoping to regain stock market losses over all that time could have been earning money elsewhere. Remember, there are lots of places to store your cash outside the stock market.

For the 2000 to 2007 period we're talking about, for example, those investors could have had their money in CDs that were insured by the Federal Deposit Insurance Corporation (FDIC) and were averaging somewhere between 3 and 5 percent annual returns. In 2007, before the last major stock market drop, a CD was delivering close to a 5 percent return.

I know. Those numbers don't sound sexy, but they produce reliable income and didn't tank like the stock markets did.

Now add everything together. When you include inflation and lost opportunity cost, it's pretty easy to see things didn't turn out as well as many investors believed. Those who were so relieved when their portfolios finally regained their original value over several years—they were kidding themselves. They did experience inflation-adjusted losses, and depending on what conservative investment options they might have pursued instead, those losses might have been significant. Let's compare this to what an investor could have earned on that $100,000: A ten-year CD at 5 percent way back in 2007 would be worth $164,866 in 2017.

Two Key Questions

Investors, especially those at or near retirement age, have some thinking to do. If you are one of those investors who came through the dot-com crash and the Great Recession, you need to consider two questions:

1. Is another major drop possible?
2. If it happens, how huge an impact might it have on you?

The first question is straightforward. An in-depth analysis of stock market history clearly suggests that a third major drop in the wake of the previous two is not only possible within the next ten years, but probable. Mull that over a second. Yes, I said probable.

The second question depends on how much attention you're paying to financial defense in your own portfolio right now.

It's easy to come up with a worst-case scenario if you or your advisor are ignoring financial defense.

Misguided Optimism

It's surprising to think that investors such as Harry or Tom and Michelle might remain committed to a "buy-and-hold" strategy in the stock market even after an experience like that, but it's not uncommon.

The main reason so many brokers and advisors virtually ignore financial defense is simply that much of the financial world is in the business of selling optimism. It starts with Wall Street, whose CEOs and shareholders have a vested interest in keeping you invested in the markets. They know you're more likely to stay invested if you're optimistic and believe the market is forever on the upswing.

From there, a majority of brokers and advisors fall dutifully into the roles of becoming "stock market cheerleaders." The only thing they lack is the pom-poms. They continue stubbornly urging you to hold on and trust in a long-term market rebound no matter what—even when there's an overwhelming amount of historical evidence out there to suggest that the secular bear market that occurred from 2000 to 2013 did not end in 2013 and still has a long way to go, and that another major drop is not only possible but probable.

I need to really stress this point. The deck is stacked against you if you are an ordinary investor. No, that doesn't mean someone will outright cheat you. They don't need to. Casinos don't need to cheat you. They know math, just as I do. They know if you keep playing long enough, the odds say they win.

Wall Street is similar. I haven't even discussed how much all of the stock maneuvering would cost your account. Management fees on your account when you are already losing 30 percent, 40 percent, or even 50 percent of its value are just one more indignity.

Harry, the retiree in my earlier example, probably spent thousands of dollars in fees in those six- to seven-year break-even markets. He lost a good chunk of his retirement money, got hit with inflation and lost opportunity cost, and had to pay for the privilege.

DAVE'S TIP NUMBER 1:
Never Gamble What You Can't Afford to Lose

What is the difference between a team owner like Stephen Ross of the Miami Dolphins and someone betting on his team? They both want the team to win and make money, but which one of them is gambling and which one isn't? Well, if you're Stephen Ross and you own the team, you have a say in choosing players and coaches, and you can have some positive effect on the game's outcome. But if you're someone betting on the team, you have no way of having any effect.

By the same token, what's the difference between Warren Buffett and the average stock investor? When Warren Buffett invests, he's usually buying controlling interests in the companies or large enough interests that he has a seat on the board of directors. In that way he can control the management and direction of the company. The average investor can't do this. All you can do is bet on the company's managers, hoping they do a good job. So that's where I see betting on a stock market as very much the same as fantasy football or any kind of gambling: You're buying fractional shares in a company in which you have no control, hoping it succeeds. In fantasy football, you're betting on a player doing well next Sunday or a game going your way. Similarly, when you buy a stock, you're betting on future profits.

And even if things go well and the company is profitable, management could still do something stupid that causes it to fall out of favor with Wall Street. The fickle whims of Wall Street can still drive the stock price down no matter what. So to me, that makes it even riskier than betting on sports or gambling in a casino. The stock market is like gambling on steroids.

I want you to remember that life isn't just about the money. It's about you. Think back to the end of 2002 and 2003 or the end of 2008 and beginning of 2009. How were you affected emotionally?

Think about the toll those downturns took on you.

1. Did you refuse to open up your statements for fear of what was inside?
2. Did you lose sleep over what the markets did on any given day?
3. In the middle of any given day that the market was plummeting, was it difficult to concentrate on anything else?
4. Did you alter your spending habits out of fear?
5. Did you pray to God that "if the market rebounds and my accounts recover, I promise I'll never, ever, play the stock market again"?

You don't have to concentrate on each answer. Just try to remember how you felt. Because I know many investors who felt the same way. Years later, they still get this awful aching in the pit of their stomachs just thinking about their financial future.

That ache is a warning. Your body is telling you something is wrong and you shouldn't ignore it. Your future isn't a casino. Sure, you can afford to throw a few dollars down on roulette or in a slot machine. You *can't* afford to have your future and your children's future crash that same way.

That's why you shouldn't gamble more than a small percentage of those hard-earned dollars following the market cheerleaders who seem to think the only direction for stocks is skyward. If you confidently answered no to all five questions, then you might be one of the lucky few who are overprotective enough by nature to be a 100 percent do-it-yourselfer.

If you are like most people, however, I'd strongly urge you to not go it alone. That means you need a guide, like in the old Westerns. Someone to get you through dangerous territory.

To help you determine if your current advisor or the one you are considering is that right kind of advisor to guide you, one who has the overprotective skills to help keep your money and your future secure, here are a few questions to ask of the advisor:

1. "For your typical client at my stage in life, what percentage of my assets would you have in common stocks or stock mutual funds versus income-generating alternatives?" (I recommend 40 percent or less.) If you are retired or seven to ten years from retirement.
2. "What percentage of assets do you tell your clients they can take annually from the portfolio while being reasonably confident that they will never run out of money?" (I recommend 4 percent or less per year.)
3. "How do you generate enough interest or dividends from the portfolio to satisfy the income needs of your clients?" (This is a very telling question. A blank stare or surprised head tilt might indicate an advisor who is not overprotective!)
4. "During each of the two market drops since 2000, how did you respond to clients who called in a panic? What did you tell them to calm their nerves?" (This is a trick question—ideally, you want to hear that clients thanked the advisor for pulling them out of the market in time and for not giving the typical Wall Street pep talk.)
5. "What major changes did you make to your client allocation model after 2003 and again after 2009?" (Again, a blank stare isn't what you want in an advisor. I recommend an advisor who is overprotective enough so that clients don't have to feel that pain of losses more than once.)

Imagine waking up tomorrow and seeing the market was collapsing. Picture telling your children that the money you had saved to help them buy a house or hold a nice wedding is now gone. Instead, now you have to worry about you. You don't have enough to worry about them.

You don't have to tell me. You'd feel awful. Like you'd let them down.

Then don't. Don't let some salesperson dictate your future.

Now, if you want to figure out how to fix your problem, how to keep from having your investments own you, then read on.

2

FINANCIAL DETAIL ORIENTATION

YOU'VE BEEN INVESTING all your life. Remember the first time one of your relatives—a grandparent or maybe a kindly aunt—slipped a few dollars into a birthday card? You felt you had hit the lottery. You were *rich*! You might not recall whether it was a birthday or a holiday, but I bet you remember how much money it was. That was the key detail.

Suddenly, the bigger questions of what to do with that money came up. Spend or save? Do you rush to buy some candy or perhaps a toy? Or save it for later to buy something nicer? Either way, your first bank account was probably a piggy bank on your dresser or maybe a hollowed-out old book.

Spend or save? Those are the same questions that have followed your investment life as you've gotten older, as you've encountered the financial milestones of your life. Remember your first real bank account? How about your first paycheck? Remember the thrill you felt deep inside? Those details have built your financial success. Learning how the world works is essential if you want to succeed.

Each step along the way of your career has been a step forward in your financial life. Getting a credit card. Taking out a loan to buy a car.

Unless you're a real estate agent, the whole process of buying a house seemed like one endless mountain of paperwork that you had to climb—contracting with the agent, offers, home inspections, closing documents, and getting a mortgage. All because you decided to invest in a house.

I know, you weren't really thinking it was an investment; it was a home. A place to put down roots and grow a family. But it was still an investment, a financial decision that impacted your life for years to come, and a world of details, any one of which could have meant disaster if handled poorly.

All of that laid the groundwork for your first real adventures in investing and trying to make a profit. There was the first mutual fund you bought. Maybe a friend recommended it, or perhaps you read about it in the *Wall Street Journal*.

Other funds followed. Then you bought a few stocks and invested in your retirement accounts. Perhaps you even signed up for an individual retirement account (IRA).

It's been a lifetime of earning and learning—a parade of details, some of which you recall and many that no longer seem so important. Now it's time to learn some more and maybe even unlearn a bit. Wall Street has been teaching you that there's only one right way to invest and that the stock market is the only game in town. Everywhere you go, you've been taught buy and hold—in movies, TV shows, and the billion or so investment books you've read.

Wall Street honchos don't want you to learn about alternatives. They don't want you to think other than what they tell you to think. They definitely don't want you to think for yourself.

I'm going to change that. Principle 2 in this book is about one of the most important things you can ever learn: getting the details right. Because investing is all about a lot of little decisions. You don't have to get them all correct, but if you don't, you'd better hope you have a financial advisor who can.

How I Developed My Eye for Details

My mom had a clear sense of what was right and what wasn't. She had one heck of a smile that I can still see. But till the day she died she made sure everyone around her knew she expected a lot. Toward the end of her life, she insisted on those standards from those who took care of her. She expected good performance from her caretakers. She was the customer and had every right to it.

She had taught me about that internal sense of right and wrong. Hers came from her incredible sense of detail. I'm not sure if it was her career training or that Mom found the right kind of job for her personality. She had worked in a couple of factory jobs, but probably her longest stint, before she got married and had me, was with Seth Thomas Clock Company as a quality control person.

Seth Thomas was one of the big names in clocks and had an excellent reputation. The clocks were built to last because Seth Thomas made quality. And they kept that quality because they were smart enough to hire detail-oriented people like my mom.

She was definitely a quality control person. I would love to have seen her at work in that job. I can just picture her going over the clocks in every way imaginable. I know how exacting she could be. She'd look and make sure the case was made correctly and that it was all nailed or glued together cleanly. Then she'd examine the face, looking for imperfections. And she'd spend several minutes checking the guts of the clock. Finally, she'd check the timing down to the second.

If you built a clock that got past my mom for quality, then you built a darn good clock.

So that's where I get my detail skills from, when it comes to quality. Now I expect the same from the people who work for me.

How My Eye for Detail Was Perfected

Seth Thomas had Mom five days a week. I had her doing quality control on me the whole time I was growing up. We lived in an apartment, so there were no outdoor chores. I had to clean the house to earn my allowance. That's where she'd teach me how to do a job correctly. She made sure I dusted everything, picked everything up, and vacuumed everything. It had to be done right. It had to be perfect. That was her way.

That taught me how to excel and how to focus on the little things. If I missed a spot dusting or vacuuming, she might not say much. Miss two or three spots and it had to be done better. It wasn't just the mistake; it was the pattern. She didn't like sloppy work. She knew I had the skills to do better, even as a young boy.

I grew up believing that there was only one way to do things—the right way. But I also learned that you can overdo it. I still remember my first math quiz. I scored an almost perfect grade on my math SATs when I took them in high school, but my first math quiz ended in disaster.

I got a 44. Out of 100.

That's right. My first math quiz in the first grade, I got 44 percent right. Some math expert I am.

The reason was because I only answered 44 percent of the questions. I was writing out the numbers perfectly like the letters on the wall above the chalkboard. It didn't matter if I finished, each one had to be perfect. The ones had to be perfectly straight. The eights a pair of perfectly stacked ovals and so on.

I ran out of time. I ended up with a bad score. And that was a lesson. Perfection is one thing, but you've got to finish. So, even in first grade, I was learning how to balance perfection with reality.

I enjoyed math. For example, one of my favorite games was while we were driving. I'd add up the numbers on the license plates as the cars were coming toward us. This is back when there were two letters and three numbers on the plates and there were fewer cars. I'd see a car with XJ946 and in my mind it was instantly XJ 19. Soon I could do basic math on the fly, faster than my classmates. When I could add them up quickly enough that it was no longer a challenge, I tried something new. Eventually, I started converting the letters to numbers. If I saw an A it was 1, a Z and it was 26, and I'd add them in. It was a whole new ball game. JL 327 wasn't JL 12, it was simply 34 (J = 10, L = 12).

To this day, if you give me any letter I can tell you where it ranks in the alphabet.

Sure, I liked math, but no single thing drove me down the career path I chose. Both my interest in finance and my counting nature added together. Multiply them with an extreme attention to detail and you end up pursuing a job in finance somewhere.

It's More Than Just the Numbers

There is more to a job—or to life!—than numbers, though I sometimes hated to admit it. Thank God I learned that. At one point, I considered becoming an insurance actuary. A friend told me, "You're going to be miserable if you end up as an actuary."

It's a good thing I listened, because actuaries just go by the numbers. And I started becoming really successful only when I was no longer just relying on numbers. For years and years, I tried to be logical about the numbers. That's the guy who's adding up numbers on license plates, the math guy. Then I realized that I needed to become more right-brained and to trust my gut instincts. (The left part of your brain is purportedly the more mathematical/logical side, and the right is supposedly the more creative side.) Most successful people have a balance between both. I think I've found that balance.

I still have an uncanny ability to look at a list of numbers and immediately identify the one that is incorrect. That's still my foundational skill set. We once had a situation in the office where someone used numbers I knew were wrong. I can always tell if it doesn't pass the sniff test. I say, "That's not right."

I hate to put people on the spot, but the number was obviously wrong. "No, we're not up by X amount." That much was obvious, but I knew exactly why the number was misinterpreted and by the amount that it was off. I don't have to get into the weeds to see that a number is wrong. I just have to pay enough attention.

I *now* use the analytics—to backstop my work. I first trust my right-brain vision and then I use the analytics as a check along the way. It's all test and measure, test and measure. It's how you run a business, especially if you had good mentors.

The Data That Shouldn't Be Ignored

The investing strategy I came up with is one that I now use at the Advisors' Academy and Sound Income Strategies. Comparatively few others use it, because they think it isn't sexy. It's not Wall Street enough for them. The investments don't usually skyrocket (or crater) overnight. Personally, I think consistent returns, low stress, and having a balanced life make for a sexy and sane combination. But that's me.

I am willing to bet it's you, and most of America too. All of us are tired of the Wall Street shuffle. We're tired of watching our mutual funds get mediocre returns while the fees keep paying some big financial firm somewhere.

We're tired of stock market initial public offerings (IPOs) that go to the elite, and by the time ordinary investors get in on them, the stocks have tanked. We're tired of a market that is tied to every single event in the world—from the crisis in the Middle East (and when isn't there a crisis in the Middle East?) to rising/falling oil prices, to who wins elections in 2016, 2018, 2020, out into infinity.

The result always seems to be that Wall Street wins and the rest of us lose or win a lot less. Doing things Wall Street's way got us the dot-com implosion. It was followed up by the crash of 2008. That's not the world any of us wants to keep our money in, but we don't know what else to do.

So I stopped playing their game. Oh, I still follow it. I still track what they do. You can't fight an enemy and ignore what they're doing. And believe me, I'm not doing this to tangle with Wall Street. I'm doing it for my clients and for you and your families.

Perspective always matters: They say the devil is in the details. If so, he's got a lot of company because everything's in the details. Your future is in the details.

Luckily, I love details.

I love them so much that I've studied them my entire career. I've already mentioned how I warned my clients to get out before the 2000 market collapse. I made that call because I follow statistics. I follow trends. Each trend is like a buffet of details.

Call up a stock market chart on your computer. Whether you want one for the Dow or the S&P, Google will oblige you. It will give you a wonderfully detailed chart showing highs and lows. It gives you one-day, five-day, and on up to five-year information. The last category is classic. It's called "Max."

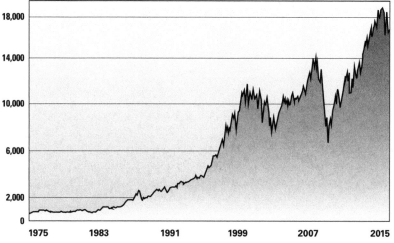

Dow Jones Industrial "MAX" 1975 to Present

(Figure 3—Dow Jones Industrial "MAX" 1975 to Present)

Source: https://finance.yahoo.com/q/hp?s=%5EDJI&a=00&b=1&c=1975&d=02&e=30&f=2016&g=d

If you're like most people, you would assume that means everything. The "Max" Google chart only goes back to 1975. Forty years of markets. That's the longest standard chart that investors can easily find on the Internet.

There's only one problem. Even your average noninvestor knows markets go back a lot further than that. Traders know it too, though lazy ones probably rely too much on information like the DJIA "Max" chart (see Figure 3).

We've been trading securities in this country since the late 1700s, and the New York Stock Exchange is almost 200 years old. That means we have a heck of a lot more market history to rely on than just the past forty years. Very few people realize this. Finding the data isn't easy. Even an aggressive search usually turns up Dow Jones data going back to 1926, and that's fifty years' more information than most websites supply. The shorter charts look impressive—it's like standing right next to a mountain (see Figure 4). The perspective changes when you see the whole history of stock mar-

Dow Jones Industrial 1926 to 2016

(Figure 4—Dow Jones Industrial 1926 to 2016)

Source: http://finance.yahoo.com/q/hp?s=%5EDJI&a=00&b=3&c=1926&d=05&e=11&f=2016&g=w

ket performance. If you want to look at the market's entire history, you need to look back almost 200 years.

Back in the 1990s before the Internet, many brokers showed customers a graph of this carefully picked data set called the "mountain chart." It covered about seventy years from 1926 on. It showed the mammoth growth of the markets. If you didn't ask too many questions, it was easy not to look more closely and hard not to just dump your money into the markets, because you had a rotten perspective.

It's more complicated than the "mountain chart" shows. If you look closely, market history suggests that it takes thirty-five years or so for the market to go full cycle. A full secular bull/bear cycle lasts approximately thirty-five years. So when brokers say, "Over the long run, the market outperforms most other asset classes," you need to ask, "How long is the long run?" You now know the answer. So, if you invest for an entire thirty-five-year period, statistically speaking, you should outperform other investments: That's the long run. But if you missed *any part of those thirty-five years* or need your money sometime during that period, you could be in trouble. So, they told you the truth, but not the *whole truth.*

A thirty-five-year investment cycle is not the kind of information you're going to glean from a forty-year stock chart. Financial advisors who might have spent their entire career getting research from the Internet might never even crack a book to show you the other 160 years of market history—or understand what those 160 years mean to you and your money. Those advisors have been fed the same bull that you have. Advisors don't get their research out of thin air. Many rely on the research from their investment firms.

Unfortunately, that perspective keeps them in the dark. Even with all the knowledge we have access to, advisors who count on their own firms for information typically can't see over that mountain.

That's why digging into the details, finding hard-to-find information, might give a person a leg up on the competition.

Where Are We Now?

Investing without a strategy is like redoing the D-Day invasion of Europe without a plan. Instead of launching one of the greatest military successes in history, you just send ships and planes and tanks and men at random and watch them get chopped to pieces. It's a nightmare of failure.

The same thing happens to your finances. Moving forward without a strategy invites disaster. You invest based on a story you read in the news or on the advice a relative or friend told you, or even worse, you blindly follow your financial advisor's recommendation. You invest when the market is at the top and pull out your money after it craters.

To avoid all that, you need a plan. But before we talk strategy, let's take a look at where we are today. We've had two consecutive market meltdowns since 2000. Each one of those drops was followed by a recovery.

Personally, I saw indicators going bad in late 1998 and knew the bubble was about to burst in the market. It did so in 2000. Sadly, my studies of the details of previous bear markets showed they typically took more than two decades to clear out.

In my October 2007 newsletter to clients, I stated my adamant belief there was going to be a second drop that could be bigger than the first drop. It began almost immediately. Six months later, I wrote that this would be the first time the government would lower the federal fund rates to zero. I said they would do unprecedented things to stimulate the economy, and they have done and continue to do so.

Now, hold on to your hat or at least your wallet. As I write this in 2016, I'm predicting a third drop.

That's right, another huge drop. Twenty fifteen and early 2016 have already been pretty much a wash. Both the Dow and S&P 500 were almost exactly breakeven during those periods.

The reason I'm publicly concerned about a third drop is simple.

In 2013, the stock market broke above its peak levels from 2000 and 2007, giving the appearance of a thirteen-year recovery period. However, if this were a permanent stock market recovery—**not a temporary, government-induced one**—we'd be breaking three world records for the stock market.

Here are three historic details that tell me the third drop is coming:

1. It would be the first time we ever recovered from a secular bear market after just thirteen years.
2. It would be the first time we recovered without having three or more major drops inside a secular bear market.
3. It would be the first time the markets recovered before the price/earnings (P/E) ratio got down into single digits. The average P/E ratio right now is almost 20—hardly close to single digits.

The Right-Brained Side of Money— or Good Old Common Sense

Those reasons are important, as I'll explain. But there's another aspect to the situation—the commonsense side of it. With all of my financial background, from my master's degree in financial planning to my CFP and CFA, what helped me draw these conclusions was simple, old-fashioned common sense.

That's my lesson to everyone. Use your common sense. Don't trust the experts just because they say so. Remember what President Ronald Reagan said: "Trust, but verify." If it doesn't pass the sniff test, don't trust it. As of 2016, when I do informational workshops, I often ask, "Do you believe that history more often than not tends to repeat itself?" Inevitably, I receive a resounding "Yes!" from my audience.

As it turns out, we have over 200 years of stock market history that says a third drop is probably on its way. Historically, the S&P 500 has to drop below its highest levels from the market peaks of 2000 and 2007. That would require almost a 30 percent drop from the all-time market highs of 2015 and 2016. However, oftentimes these drops get sequentially larger. That doesn't always happen, but it has. Remember, the second drop that we endured during the financial crisis was worse than the first. And the first was pretty awful, especially if you were in tech stocks. Will the third one be even worse than the second? If so, that could result in a drop of more than 67 percent. That's right, somewhere between 30 and 67 percent or more!

Let's assume a third drop would take us back down to the lows of March 2009. Back then the S&P 500 was at 676. That's a 67 percent drop, from the peak to that level.

Picture for a moment losing 67 percent of everything you have in the stock market. Now imagine everyone you know lost the same. It would devastate personal finances, businesses, and more—even worse than 2008. And that was the worst economic cataclysm since the Great Depression.

Are you prepared for that? Are your investments?

In 2016, some people might mistakenly be thinking, "What if market momentum keeps growing? What if we get another 10 percent to 20 percent upside before the third drop? I'd hate to forfeit that potential growth."

Think of it this way. Imagine you and I walk into a casino together to gamble. Americans love to gamble. We know it well—from Super Bowl to the NCAA tournament to the Triple Crown. We bet a lot. Now picture us in that casino. There's a table where if you win, you win $20; but if you lose, you lose $67. Are you going to play at that table?

Of course not.

That's where I see the market today.

Instead of trying to squeeze out the last 10 percent or 20 percent of the upside, it's time to use common sense. That means you need to be careful. I believe institutional money right now is nervous because they see what I see. I think they have one finger on the trigger, ready to target which areas or markets to get rid of. I believe that's why the markets didn't do much of anything in 2015 or early 2016. Too much institutional money has gotten the jitters.

It's like a game of musical chairs when you were a kid. The music stops and you're stuck without a chair. Who's going to be stuck without a chair? The average mom-and-pop investor or the big institutional investor? Mom-and-pop investors are going to lose every time. Institutional investors have a permanent seat at the table, so they won't be left without a chair.

Occasionally it can pay to take a risk if you are a risk taker and have time on your side. For example, if you got in during 2009, at the bottom, and sold in 2013 when the markets reestablished their high-water mark from 2000 and 2007, you would have made a lot of money. But if you followed your broker's advice and stayed in after 2013 when the market went above its previous high—1,570 in the S&P—yes, you would have profited even more, though you would have pushed your luck.

You can play Russian roulette once, maybe twice, and you're okay. But if you pull the trigger six times with the same gun, you are going to lose. The results won't be pretty. I remember one of the famous Clint Eastwood lines: "You feelin' lucky?" *No one is that lucky.*

How was it that I was able to figure this out in the past? Was it because of all my credentials?

No, not one helped. Common sense did the trick. But it helps if you know the details of market history, and you believe it is unlikely the stock market is about to break three world records.

World Record Number One—
The first time our country has recovered from a secular bear market after only thirteen years

If you believe the saying "History repeats itself," you are not alone. That's an important adage to keep in mind when it comes to saving and investing for retirement because it allows you to get a glimpse into the future by knowing about the past.

The fact is, the stock market has been repeating itself consistently enough throughout its history. That lets us see repeatable long-term patterns, or market "biorhythms." Those are important to recognize and understand when it comes to building a smart, defensive investment strategy.

First, you need to understand something about the Wall Street "truth" most brokers like to tell when talking about the stock market: "Over the long run, the stock market outperforms most other asset classes." Again, it's true, but it's not the whole truth. Most people have probably been told that the market averages about a 9 percent annual return over the very long run. It's not quite that simple. The way that breaks down over the long term is that 2 to 3 percent of this return comes from stock dividends, and 6 to 7 percent comes from capital appreciation. In other words, investors get a 6 to 7 percent average growth rate over the very long run.

That may sound pretty good, but only if you are in the markets for every second of that very long run. As you might recall, that's thirty-five years.

Let me explain something about how "averages" are determined and why they can be misleading. If I told you that my business partner and I jogged "an average of" ten miles per week, you might be impressed, until I explained that my partner actually jogs twenty miles and I don't jog at all. Now, together we do still "average" that ten miles, so I did tell the truth—it was just not the whole truth.

The numbers can't lie. But how they are used can. It's a great example of lies, damn lies, and statistics. Statistics are always the worst. You went from imagining my partner and me as regular runners to envisioning one of us as running nearly a marathon a week and the other living life as a "couch potato."

That's how that "average" growth rate is determined for the stock market. The way the 6 to 7 percent breaks down over the long run is that there are huge periods of time where the market experiences extreme volatility but the net result is zero growth—the exact kind of growth we experienced in 2015.

Then there are huge periods of time where the market does very well, averaging over 10 percent growth annually, and often in the 12 to 15 percent range. Factor zero with that high range, and there is your 6 to 7 percent average return.

Market Cycle Details

So what exactly are these huge periods of time that alternate between growth and stagnation? They're the consistently repeatable long-term market cycles. They consist of one long-term secular bull market (growth) period and one long-term secular bear (zero-growth) period, which collectively comprise one market biorhythm, approximately thirty-five years. Here is your detailed history lesson:

From 1899 to about 1921—based on the most commonly available stock market indicators from that time—the market experienced tons of volatility. Big gains, huge drops; but in the end, all the good and bad years over that long stretch of time washed each other out, resulting in a period of zero growth over twenty-two years.

Imagine the nightmare of investing for twenty-two years and having little or nothing to show for it. That's the reality I'm discussing.

Right after that period came an eight-year stretch—from 1921 to 1929—which represented, at that time, the best decade we had ever seen for the stock market.

Now you understand why we call those years the "Roaring Twenties." It wasn't just flapper dresses and bootleg whiskey. The 1920s flowed more with cash than with illegal alcohol.

All that came to an abrupt halt, of course, with the stock market crash of 1929 and the start of the Great Depression. But an interesting note ignored by most history books is that "The Crash" actually signaled the start of something very much like that 1899 to 1921 period of zero growth.

From 1929 to 1954 the market again experienced tons of volatility—big gains and huge drops that ultimately washed each other out, resulting in a twenty-five-year stretch of zero growth. That encompassed the whole Depression era, World War II, and a good chunk of the postwar era. Even with all of the soldiers coming home from the war, it took nine years for things to get going again.

Then came another long stretch where the market did incredibly well: 1954 to 1966. The Eisenhower era was when America was totally on top of its game. Unemployment was very low, and people were making good incomes and living well.

If you've been paying attention, I bet you know what happens next.

In 1966, markets started to turn again. Once more we entered a long cooling-off period. This time it lasted almost seventeen years, from 1966 to 1982. Once more, the market had major ups and downs that ultimately canceled each other out. The result was zero growth over all that time. For example, the Dow Jones Industrial Average hit 1,000 in 1966, and in 1982 it was still at 1,000. That was also the only downturn of less than twenty years.

Then—right on schedule—the market again took off. We enjoyed the best bull market we've ever seen in U.S. history, which lasted eighteen years until 2000. In that time the Dow went from 1,000 to almost 12,000, a twelvefold increase that culminated with the high-flying 1990s.

What's even more interesting is that these biorhythms go back even before 1899, to the very beginning of a primitive stock market in 1792. Throughout all of market history, we've consistently seen extended good times (long-term secular bull markets) followed by extended bad times (long-term secular bear markets) that resulted in zero overall growth.

That takes us to the twenty-first century. After enjoying the best bull market in our country's history for eighteen years, everything turned again. It happened right on schedule in 2000. The century started with another major market drop, and in the following thirteen years we experienced tons of volatility and two major drops that have wiped out previous gains.

Let's look closer at these alternating historical cycles and ask ourselves: How long is the average secular bear market, and how long is the average secular bull market? On average, these long bear cycles have typically lasted twenty years or more, while the bull periods have averaged slightly less.

That means, as I explained before, that it takes about thirty-five years for the market to go through one full cycle.

Statistically speaking, if you have money that you know for sure you're not going to need or want to spend for thirty-five years, you should, in theory, be able to put it in the stock market and have it outperform most other investments.

That's because, over the very long run, the market has averaged a 9 percent return.

Now you know just what it means when your broker says "in the long run." Unfortunately, I don't come across too many people in a position to just sit on their nest egg, or even part of it, for three and a half decades.

World Record Number 2—
The first time our country has recovered from a secular bear market without having three or more cyclical bear markets within

Another important detail to understand about history is that every long-term secular bear market cycle we've been through has included at least three major market drops. Our current secular bear cycle has had only two drops as of this writing.

It's also common that each sequential drop has gotten larger than the one previous. Here again, let me hammer home this point: Our current secular bear cycle, so far, has been true to form, as the second drop was indeed larger than the first.

Now we're waiting for the third shoe to drop. Just to match the last drop, the market would have to experience a 68 percent decline from its all-time peak.

World Record Number 3—
The first time our country has recovered from a secular bear market without P/E ratios being in the single digits

Here is the third detail as to why history says the markets are due for a big correction—P/Es. That's simply the market value per share/earnings per share of a stock. By comparing these two performance measures in one stock and then measuring the ratio alongside that of another stock, you can often learn which stock is a better buy. As a very general rule of thumb, the stock with the lower price-to-earnings ratio is the more attractive because it is considered undervalued. Remember the goal is always to buy low and sell high.

For instance, let's say you have Stock A selling at $30 per share and the company has earnings of $1 per share. Compare that to

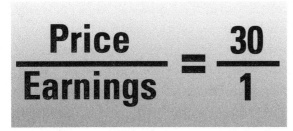

$$\frac{Price}{Earnings} = \frac{30}{1}$$

(Figure 5—Price to Earnings Ratio)

Stock B selling at $50 a share and whose corporate earnings are $5 a share. Which one is the bargain?

The first stock is substantially cheaper, but it's no bargain. The second company, with the higher-priced stock, is actually the better deal (see Figure 5).

That's because 50 divided by 5 is a 10 P/E, while 30 divided by 1 is a 30 P/E. Of course, 10 is lower than 30, so Stock B, with the lower price-to-earnings ratio, is better.

It's important to remember that there's a lot more to consider than P/E ratios when choosing which stock to buy, but it's definitely something you want to understand.

As it turns out, both individual stocks and the market overall have a P/E ratio. If you keep track of the overall ratio it can give you a good indication of when stock market levels are generally too high and ready to drop.

Let me explain a bit more about P/Es in the simplest way I know. Have you ever bought for your child or grandchild a pair of pants that was too big? It's a common occurrence, and when it happens you have two easy options, short of the hassle of returning them. One, you can throw the pants in the wash and try to shrink them. Or two, you can just sit back knowing that child or grandchild will eventually grow into them.

This same phenomenon applies when the price of stocks becomes overinflated in relationship to annual corporate profits. If you can learn to recognize when it's happening, that knowledge can go a long way toward helping you make smart, safe savings and investment decisions—decisions built on the right principles.

This is exactly what I observed in the late 1990s when I recognized that our current secular bear market was about to begin. At that time, the average P/E ratios exceeded 30, which meant that each dollar invested was buying just three cents of earnings or annual profits. To put that into perspective, you would have been earning about 3 percent on your investments (1/30) when during that same period you could have taken some of the same money and bought an FDIC-insured CD with no risk and earned 5 percent. What I saw started to worry me. The overall price of stocks was becoming overinflated relative to actual corporate profits—just like a pair of pants too big for a young child.

I understood from my knowledge of market history and my grasp of the basic financial ratios that one of two things was likely to happen to correct this growing imbalance. The first would have been even more devastating to my clients. Overall stock prices had to shrink by 75 percent, meaning the Dow would drop below 3,000 (it was over 11,000 at the time). Or we could slip into a significant and prolonged period of market volatility while we waited for corporate profits to grow into these baggy price levels.

I knew the odds were slim that the market would shrink by that much. That kind of drop doesn't happen often, thankfully. That was when I concluded we were sitting on the cusp of a brand-new, twenty-plus-year secular bear market.

I wasn't sure when it would officially start, but I feared it would be soon. This was based partly on my understanding of stock market biorhythms and past secular market cycles. But I also had an understanding of the basic stock market formula: price-to-earnings ratio.

P/E History

Let's see what history tells us about P/E ratios when we look at long-term secular market cycles of the past. Whenever we've come to the end of a secular bull market cycle—be it in the late 1920s, the mid-1960s, or the late 1990s—P/E ratios have typically been near or above 30. So, history tells us, that's a warning sign.

Why a P/E of 30? Because that's the point where the imbalance in the price-to-earnings formula is bordering on ridiculous. That's exactly how things looked in the late 1990s when so many people were still buy-and-hold happy despite this crazy imbalance.

Look at it this way. Suppose you decided to buy an ice cream parlor and the owner wanted a cool $3 million for it. You knew the business consistently earned $100,000 annually. That's a P/E ratio of 30, just like when the stock was only $30 a share and earnings were $1.

It also means it would take you thirty years to recoup your investment and, hopefully, start turning a profit. I bet that FDIC-insured CD is sounding better all the time. You could have bought it, earned more in less time, and never had to dig into a single carton of Rocky Road.

Now look at the opposite end of the P/E spectrum. Typically, toward the end of a secular bear market, P/E ratios slip below 10, very often into the 6-to-8 range. Historically, that's a key signal that the next secular bull market cycle of steady growth is about to begin. This has not yet happened since the secular bear market began in the year 2000.

So where are overall stock market P/E ratios now? As of 2016 the P/E ratio of the S&P 500 index is almost 20, more than twice the level needed to signal the end of this secular bear market cycle.

Secular bear markets like the one we're in right now typically last twenty years or more because that's how long it takes for P/E ratios to drop from 30 to the 6-to-8 range. Again, that generally happens in one of two ways: Either stock market levels suddenly drop by 75 percent (which hardly ever happens) or corporate earnings slowly quadruple and grow into the inflated stock prices—just like a child might grow into that oversized pair of pants.

To "slowly" quadruple usually takes twenty years or more—with the market fluctuating wildly the whole time.

Clearly, P/E ratios can serve as a detail that indicates where we stand in a secular market cycle. It's not the only indicator.

It bears repeating that we would have to break all three records regarding the stock market if the gains over the last three years were an indication of a permanent recovery instead of a temporary, government-induced one. Market history strongly suggests there will be at least a 30 percent drop to below 2013 levels from the highs the market hit in the middle of 2015 and early 2016, and it could be as much as 68 percent or more.

Hidden Realities of the Market

At this point you should be wondering why when you hear financial analysts on television talking about a "bear market" they never say anything about it lasting twenty years or more. Most analysts talk "bear markets" that last two or three years at most.

The analysts aren't lying. They're just showing you a limited perspective based on an alternate definition of a bear market: "a cyclical bear market."

Remember, one of the key characteristics of a long-term secular bear market is volatility. There are a lot of ups and downs, negating each other, resulting in zero growth. These ups and downs are called "cyclical" bear and bull markets and occur within longer-term secular cycles.

Wall Street analysts and the mainstream media would rather focus on them when they talk about market conditions.

Why? It's all tied to what Wall Street does and doesn't want the average investor to know. Wall Street insiders like to speak optimistically as often as possible. More than half of all Americans aren't invested in the markets; no stocks, no individual retirement accounts (IRAs), and no 401(k)s. Wall Street needs to keep the rest of us as optimistic and fully invested as it can.

Wall Street bigwigs know they can make more money because more people will invest in their products if people are optimistic and think the markets are going to do well. The reality is that if Wall Street pundits talk about short-term cyclical cycles, they can speak optimistically about the markets more often. And who doesn't want to be part of an up market? After all, what sounds better, "The stock market should be recovering in the next year or two," or "The stock market should take twenty more years to recover"?

It's easy to understand why Wall Street would prefer to talk about short-term cycles and ignore the very existence of long-term secular cycles. What do you think might have happened to a Wall Street CEO if in 2000 he had publicly forecast that a twenty-plus-year secular bear market was just starting and advised his sales force against selling any more stocks or mutual funds?

He probably would have been out of a job—in less time than it took you to read what I wrote.

Optimism is great, but realism is more important.

That leads us to the obvious question: Is it possible that this will be the first time in nearly 200 years that the stock market will recover after only thirteen years of a secular bear market cycle? And will it do so *without* a third major drop?

Anything is possible, of course. But the lessons of stock market history clearly tell us that it's not likely.

The Right-Brained Detail

Another fact is that most people don't get serious about saving and investing for retirement until their late forties or early fifties.

With average life expectancies in the low eighties, that means most people are serious about their retirement investments for about the last thirty-five years of life. Interestingly, that's the same length of time it takes a combined secular bull-bear market cycle, or one market biorhythm, to run its course.

Coincidence? I don't believe so. We tend to think we are victims of these cycles when the reality is that each generation creates them.

Do you remember your parents giving you advice based on the bad decisions or mistakes that they made? Of course you do.

Did you take their advice every time? Of course you didn't.

Unfortunately, human nature dictates to a large extent that we learn through our own mistakes. This applies to investing mistakes as well as the other ones we make in life.

The common mistake each generation repeats is letting greed take over during good times. Every generation thinks it's smart enough to avoid that mistake. They're wrong every time. The result creates speculative asset bubbles by driving stock prices to highs not supported by economic fundamentals.

Every generation gets greedy to the point where asset prices get overblown until everything comes crashing down.

What Options Remain?

We can stay out of the market and wait for corporate earnings to grow into overinflated stock prices and for this generation's secular bear market to end. History suggests this could take several more years. It's essential to recognize that "buy and hold" doesn't work in a secular bear market. It works great in a secular bull market, but in a secular bear market it just puts you on a long roller-coaster ride that ends in zero net portfolio growth. Beyond that, you can take one of two roads:

1. **Aggressive**—Use a tactical allocation strategy in which you have a manager make wholesale moves in and out of the market to take advantage of the cyclical bull and bear markets within the long-term secular bear market cycle. This is risky, expensive in terms of management fees, and generally not likely to work very well in a secular bear market. It's essentially market timing. Let's face it—if it were easy, we'd all be doing it. My own research of market timing professionals shows more luck than science.

2. **Sane**—Stay out of the stock market altogether in a secular bear market and invest for income instead of growth. Forget about getting that last 10 percent upside of the market; protect what you have and go for steady results.

When you cross your fingers and toes hoping for capital appreciation or gains, the result sometimes turns into depreciation or losses.

> Building your wealth by receiving predictable interest and dividends from your investments is what I call a bird-in-the-hand approach.

Investing for interest or dividends is more of a "bird-in-the-hand" approach. It generates income you can spend if you're retired or that you can reinvest in order to grow your portfolio organically, or "the old-fashioned way," with far less worry over damaging losses that could impact your life and sideline your retirement plans. The point with many income-based strategies is that your income stays the same even if the investment itself goes up or down in value. That protects you as you get older and rely more on investment income to pay your bills.

There are a lot of details to know if you are going to go it alone. One needs knowledge of economics, both macro and micro; accounting; and corporate finance. In many ways, it's more challenging than simply choosing a mutual fund with a five-star rating. Whereas it's possible for a do-it-yourself investor to learn these details, that's a lot to master on your own. An alternative is to contact a qualified financial advisor who specializes in the universe of non–stock market alternatives designed to generate income through interest and dividends. But finding an advisor who truly has that specialty isn't easy.

You can't just let your money sit and hope it does better. You need to take control of your financial life to know enough that you can figure out who is best suited to help you. It's one of the most important decisions you can make, and you can use all of the details in this book to help.

DAVE'S TIP NUMBER 2:
Get Down to the Details—or Find Someone Who Will

Here are some self-analysis questions to determine if you possess the core value of detail orientation:

1. Do you struggle to calculate the tip when you go to a restaurant or do you do it in your head?
2. Do you keep a budget—at home and maybe at work, too?
3. Do you know what your investments are worth right now?

4. When did you first notice your investment accounts dropping in value during the financial crisis? (If you noticed on October 10, 2007, that means that you are detail-oriented, because that was the first day of the market drop from the new record the S&P had created from the day before. If you noticed on October 31—when you got your month-end statement—you may not be as detail-oriented as you think. If you noticed on December 31, with your year-end statement, then "Houston, we have a problem."[1])

5. Have you ever bought a stock or mutual fund based on a tip from a friend or family member without reviewing research or reports? Or, have you bought an investment based on a star-rating system? (If you have, you may not be as detail-oriented as you think.)

6. How do you (or did you) make allocation decisions on your 401(k), 403(b), or 457 plan investments? Do you pull research reports on a regular basis or simply look at the previous quarter returns to make your decisions? Or do you not pay much attention to the relative performance between funds?

If those questions are simple for you, then you might just be detail-oriented enough to take the lessons in this book and right your own financial ship. The thing is, I bet you answered, "No" to at least one of those questions. Don't be shy. It's just you and me talking now. Not everyone is as compulsive about numbers as I am.

Numbers are hard for many people. This might be the case for you, or it might not. But it sure is for most Americans.

Nearly two-thirds of Americans say that math is difficult. Three

---

1   http://english.stackexchange.com/questions/275984/houston-we-may-have-a-problem-here-meaning

in ten say they'd rather clean the bathroom than do math. A lot of people would rather clean the toilet than figure a tip[1]. If that's you, be honest with yourself. It's not embarrassing to hate numbers. But it's dangerous not to admit it, at least to yourself. Remember, I'm here to help, so I'll be honest right back. You can't manage your own finances if you can't figure out how much to tip your waiter. There, we said it. The world didn't end just because of a little honesty.

On the other hand, you may be someone who loves math. But skill with numbers in one context doesn't necessarily translate to an aptitude for investing.

We all have our skills. Maybe you've built a business or raised an amazing family and achieved huge things you can be proud of. But there isn't one of us who can do everything. I love my car, but I have a mechanic fix it. I love my boat even more, but I'm not the one changing the oil on her. I'm just not good at those things.

If you don't have that skill set, then you need to start picturing having someone help you who does have it.

It's as natural as calling a plumber for a burst pipe. The only thing you should worry about is whether to call that plumber before or after it bursts. If you wait, then maybe nothing bad happens. Or maybe the pipes tear open on a cold winter night and your floor is ruined. Waiting is risky.

In choosing a financial advisor, just like in hiring a plumber, you want someone who has the certifications, the references, and a personality you can deal with.

Here are a few questions to ask your current or prospective financial advisor regarding detailed orientation:

1. "When did you start to call your clients during the financial crisis to let them know the market had peaked and

---

1 "In a New Survey, Americans Say, We're Not Good at Math,'" *Change the Equation*, http://changetheequation.org/press/new-survey-americans-say-%E2%80%9Cwe%E2%80%99re-not-good-math%E2%80%9D"

was sliding?" (Remember, through my newsletter to my clients, I let everyone know my concerns in the first week of October 2007.)

2. "What is your definition of bull and bear market cycles?" (Does your advisor make a distinction between secular and cyclical market cycles?)

3. "How do you do your research?" (Pay close attention to the answer. For instance, when advisors are using a business model that is based on mutual funds, do they mention things like looking at the fund's standard deviation or the fund manager's alpha? Or if their business model includes individual securities, do they look at year-over-year earnings per share growth, debt-to-equity ratios, or coverage ratios? Advisors who give more generic answers may not be as detail-oriented as they would like you to believe. Many financial advisors simply glance at S&P, Moody's, or Morningstar ratings, not the details.)

But those things are only to get started. It's clear that you need an advisor who can be detailed where you aren't, who can track your finances so you don't have to. And that's just the beginning.

3

FINANCIAL DILIGENCE

Diligence Requires Patience and Determination

Sherlock Holmes is one of the greatest characters in fiction. You can find him in books, in movies, and on TV. The Baker Street detective has appeared in so many films that he's been portrayed by some of the finest actors in history—Basil Rathbone, Stewart Granger, Sir Michael Caine, Sir Ian McKellen, and even today's hot properties of Robert Downey Jr. and Benedict Cumberbatch.

What made a guy with a magnifying glass and a funny hat so popular? His diligence.

In most every portrayal of Holmes I've ever seen, people turn to him when they are baffled by a case. Scotland Yard inspectors look to him as the greatest mind of his age to bail them out. But Holmes isn't really an action hero. He doesn't find two threads of a story, grab a machine gun, and go killing bad guys.

He investigates. He analyzes. He looks over every scene for clues. He's persistent, meticulous, and kind of annoying. It's easy to imagine Holmes looking closely at the scene of a murder, taking in every detail, staring at the crowd standing nearby, searching for clues. If a clue had 423 possible results, Holmes was the man who would consider every single one.

In this day of Google searches and Internet lists, we're lucky when someone looks beyond a top ten. Holmes was the man who would solve a problem even if the solution was number 423.

I think of Holmes when I think of the kind of work top investment advisors perform. We can't be slipshod. We can't recommend a stock simply on a whim. And our market analysis needs to be stronger, because a bad market can take down even the best of stocks.

We need to grab our magnifying glasses, put on our funny hats, and get to work. In the words of Sherlock Holmes, "The game's afoot."

Be Exceptional—and Determined

Success is an exception, so be exceptional.
—MALTI BHOJWANI, MULTI COACHING INTERNATIONAL

Sports fans know this expression as "Go big, or go home."

In the field of investing, there's no one who goes bigger than Warren Buffett. His Berkshire Hathaway group has mustered what *Forbes* called "an absolutely staggering gain of 751,113 percent" in its fifty years of existence.

Put another way: A $1,000 investment in early 1965 would be worth over $15 million today. That's what being *exceptional* truly means.

It's easy to understand when you dig into Buffett's five factors of success. Perhaps the first is the most important of all: "Enjoy the game." Buffett does something he enjoys. That means he does it better than someone who hates it. If you are a "do it yourself" investor and absolutely love it, consider yourself blessed. Like Buffett, you have the potential to be very good at it. If you don't love it, then delegate the duty to an advisor who does.

It's this kind of inspired thinking that has many businesspeople watching Buffett's moves for guidance. But they focus too much on each action and need to remember the essence of what he is all about.

Excellence. That's what Warren Buffett is synonymous with. And it's something everyone in business needs to demand.

How I Learned the Difference between Diligent and Workaholic

I used to believe excellence was a direct function of the hours I put in. Work an eight-hour day and you are just scratching by. Work ten or twelve hours and you might be doing okay. You're starting to move away from the pack. I figured you had to work at least fourteen hours a day to really succeed.

When I was in my midtwenties, I was so goal-oriented I would work from 7 a.m. to as late as 9 or 10 p.m. This is part of how I found success at the beginning. I simply threw my body at the problem. I figured if I worked more than everyone else, I'd do better.

I became a machine. I'd set my coffeepot at night. (This is back when you had the timer with a dial on the wall and you had to plug it in. The timer wasn't part of the pot. We weren't that high tech then.) I'd set the timer up to go off at a certain time. I'd get up, race through a shower. Then I'd take my coffee and throw ice cubes in it. I'd swill it down, ready to start another day.

Then I'd put in an incredibly long day. I'd be there before anyone else. I'd work through lunch most days. Cold-calling in the financial business is tough. You are literally calling people you have never met and who don't even know who you are. It's hard work just to get people to talk to you. And I'd keep on calling after we closed, calling as long as I could. If I called a house and didn't get the person I wanted, I'd ask how late I could call. I'd keep calling until I wasn't allowed. By 9 or 9:30 p.m., you can't call people anymore. It's too late for business.

Sometimes, after 9:30, I'd go to the gym or to the local pub to meet more people and have the potential for face-to-face prospecting. Eventually, when I couldn't do anything more, I'd go home.

It was a grind, and I know that kind of extreme pace routine can be hard to relate to. I was pushing myself to the limit, sometimes past it. I needed to hit the bed almost as soon as I got home or I wouldn't have enough rest to do it again the next day.

I figured out my system. I kept a few beers in the refrigerator. I'd go in and get two of them. I'd slam those two beers down, barely tasting them.

The goal wasn't to get drunk or even tipsy. The idea was for it to help me sleep.

And then I'd head right upstairs to bed and collapse, falling right to sleep. I didn't waste a second. It was my own system for success.

Thank God I finally learned there's a lot more to success than just abusing your body every day. I was right about the hard work. Hard work pays off. But it's a lot more than that. It is diligence, sticking to every project, being persistent, digging and digging until you get the answers. Not always the answers you want, mind you, but the answers you need. Over time, diligence took over my workaholic streak. My clients and I are better for it.

Now my morning routine is saner. I'm no longer the hour machine, but I still drink coffee the same way. Only now, after I mix the black coffee with the ice cubes and I swill it down, I get right on the elliptical machine for my cardio. That gets my blood going. By the time I'm done a half hour later, the caffeine's there, the blood's going, and I'm ready for my day.

What Do Warren Buffet and Uncle Bill Have in Common?

On some level, I feel that as long as I keep moving, I'm fine. I do all the exercise, all the work, because I don't want to stop. When you get to a point where you can't push yourself anymore, I'm convinced it's because you stopped demanding so much of yourself. You stopped expecting yourself to excel.

And as I get older, I think that if I never stop, there's never going to be a day where yesterday I could do it and today I can't.

So you never stop. You just keep going like the Energizer Bunny.

That's the reason my uncle Bill, at age 85, rides a bike and swims in the ocean. Because he never stopped. He never gave in and never gave up. I want to be like him. He does it every day of his life.

Warren Buffett, at age 85, thinks about investments every day. Not because he needs the money, but because he loves investing. He also never stopped. I also want to be like him.

For me, a lot of that work ethic comes from my mom. She was always driving herself and always driving me. She instilled in me the same attitude about work. That gave me the foundation to want to not just achieve but overachieve. To excel.

Every one of us needs to find a path to excellence. Striving to do the best you can doesn't just happen. You have to study what you do. Own up to your failures and revel in your successes. Diligence helps you get to the point where you expect excellence of yourself at all times. When it comes to your money, that excellence comes from your or your advisor's willingness to do the necessary research and analysis to help you make the right decisions with your money. But this diligence has to be consistent. One bad decision can wipe out all the gains of three good decisions. Diligence means consistency.

Business Diligence

I'm ashamed to admit it, but there was a period early on in my career when I fell into the trap of accepting mediocrity, even though it wasn't in my (or my mom's) DNA.

For a while, I listened to others, people who didn't have my drive. They didn't share the vision or never-give-up attitude, the I-know-this-is-what-I-want belief. They didn't agree with my get-out-of-my-way-I'm-going-to-get-it-or-die-trying business model.

Some in the company told me that I was asking too much of people. "They're employees, not business owners," they reminded me. "They're never going to be as diligent as you want."

For a while, things got to the point where I let a few people talk me into thinking, "Well, maybe you're never going to have that team that you want. You're never going to be able to motivate people to fire on all cylinders like that." They had me accept a little bit of mediocrity.

It worked for a while, when the company was smaller. But it was killing me. Every time there'd be a discussion of how to do a new project or a debate on how to try a particular strategy, my employees would defer to me. "Dave, you're the best at that," they would whine, delegating up, piling more on that wagon that I had to pull.

It became almost too much. The wagon got too heavy for me to pull.

Yet, out of necessity, I became a one-man team of Clydesdales pulling my company in the direction I knew it needed to go, dragging it step by step toward excellence.

I gradually realized the situation and began to fix it. I wasn't satisfied with mediocrity. I wanted excellence. The company needed it, and our clients sure had a right to expect it. I needed to find others as diligent as myself.

Things began to turn around a few years ago when I started looking for new department directors. I knew I needed the best. Good enough wasn't going to get it done. I needed people who wouldn't just follow my lead. I needed directors who could excel on their own but who could also follow my lead and not turn into a bunch of "lone rangers."

I got more serious than ever about excellence. I restarted my journey toward success. I began to study it, focus on it, and consume it.

I learned about *kaizen*, the Japanese strategy for excellence. Kaizen means "change for better," and it is a way to look at all the activities of a company, from employees all the way up to the CEO.

The goal is to streamline a business, to make it better, stronger, and more efficient. The Japanese learned how efficient American businesses were and, after World War II, decided to remake their industry to become even better.

I applied kaizen to my business.

All of that has made me an ongoing student of excellence. I became an NLP-certified trainer. Neuro-linguistic programming, or NLP, "encompasses the three most influential components involved in producing human experience: neurology, language, and programming."[1] It's all about helping people excel.

More excellence.

My staff from top to bottom have noticed the change, but it has not unfolded without bumps in the road. Fairly recently I had an encounter with one of our divisional directors who just pushed me too far. He was a highly paid person who had different beliefs on how things should be done and repeatedly wasn't doing what I asked him to do.

He was a great player, but wasn't excelling on our team. I finally confronted him and told him what needed to be done to remain part of my team.

---

1 Robert B. Dilts, "What Is NLP?" NLP University, http://www.nlpu.com/NewDesign/NLPU_WhatIsNLP.html

Shortly afterward, I decided the best thing to do was to trade that player to another team. That closed the door on mediocrity for me, not just this time but forever.

The problem is "experts" have a strong will. They will push you in the direction they think is right. You need to be stronger so that they don't drown out that inner voice that you know is correct. It's the same strength you need to have when stock market cheerleaders try to push you toward risk in your investment portfolio.

But whatever you do, don't ever quit, don't ever give up!

Diligence + Persistence = Success

I've always been much happier when I demanded excellence of myself and others—no matter how much it cost me, no matter how difficult. I've always felt satisfied when I drove myself, when I took the hard road to try to excel.

I used to run that hard road—literally. I liked running. It's a solo sport and it lets you think a lot. You get to add the numbers on the license plates as they pass you on your run. So it was right up my alley. I ran a lot and I really did enjoy it. I got to compete against myself, which I liked.

I got to push myself.

I decided to run a marathon and go a full twenty-six miles. I gradually increased my distances over six months and got to the point where I thought I could do a twenty-mile run, and that's the territory you need to be in to stretch yourself and go the distance for a full marathon.

My body decided it didn't want to cooperate. All of a sudden I started getting a bad hip pointer and that meant pain. I was in so much agony that I couldn't even run a quarter mile. This happened only a few weeks before the race.

I went to the doctor, eager to have him fix me up for the marathon. He asked me if I had ever had a hip injury. "Of course not," I responded.

The doctor smiled. That was the right answer. I was going to be fine. He just told me to rest it. I was thirty-one years old, still young enough that I wasn't worried about a minor injury. I figured he was right. Rest was all I needed.

It was a busy time in my life. I was really focused on the race but only barely focused on my health. I had totally forgotten that when I was fourteen, I hurt myself at the gym.

It was an awful accident. I tore all the tendons and ligaments in one hip. The doctor at the time told me I was never going to run again. "You're screwed," I think he said to underscore his point.

Well, of course, I proved him wrong. I got better. I got so much better, in fact, that I forgot all about that accident. It had been years.

So I did what my new doctor told me. I rested it and finally got better. A week before the marathon I finally felt well enough to do my long practice run. Most marathoners would say that's foolish. It's too soon before the race.

What did I know? I was determined to race and nothing was going to stop me. I came down to Florida from Connecticut and ran the twenty-mile confidence-building run there. The idea is if you can run twenty miles, you can make yourself run the last six miles. It's a psychological boost.

It was January, and running in the northern cold wouldn't help me prepare anyhow. The marathon I was training for was in Bermuda later that month. I figured if I'm going to do a marathon, I'm going to do it someplace nice. Someplace warm.

Strangely, my hip didn't bother me on the twenty-mile run. I dodged a bullet. I went back to Connecticut and then got very sick. The doctor told me I had bronchitis and it was getting into my lungs. He summed it up succinctly: "You shouldn't run the marathon."

He didn't know me very well. I asked him, "Doc, am I going to die if I run the marathon?"

The doctor didn't seem to understand the question, or didn't want to act like he did. He answered me back: "You really can't run the marathon."

We did this like a comedy sketch, back and forth. I asked him two or three times and he gave me similar answers each time. Finally, I had enough. I said, "Doc, Doc, listen to me carefully. What's the mathematical probability that I'm going to die if I run this marathon?"

He thought for a second, one of those long doctor pauses that we all hate. Then he said, "Well, you're probably not going to die." I shook his hand and told him that was all I needed to know.

I was determined to run this marathon. Bronchitis or not. Hip pointer or not. I trained for it, so I was doing it.

The marathon was Saturday and I was shaving it close, flying out Friday morning. I didn't have a lot of spare time. I had a 6 a.m. flight from Connecticut in January.

Of course, it was snowing, too. I was determined to make my flight, so my better half and I got to the airport early. We were sitting there watching the list of flights turn red, one by one. That meant they were canceled.

I looked out the window and it was snowing heavily. I was worried our flight was in trouble. The only good thing was that we were flying south, out of the storm. They loaded us on the plane. We were all excited. Bermuda, here we come.

And they closed the airport.

The flight crew pulled us back off the plane and my wife looked at me and said, "It isn't meant to be. You have bronchitis, there's a snowstorm. Just accept it."

I don't "just accept" things well. I said, "The hell with all that." I was getting to Bermuda by any means necessary. We left my car in the parking garage and hailed a cab. I told the tired cabbie, "Take us to Hartford. Take us to the train station."

Now she looked at me like I was crazy and said, "What are you doing?" I smiled and explained that we were taking the train as far south as we needed, until we got to where there was no more snow.

The train took us all the way to Baltimore. We grabbed another cab and headed to the airport. This time we were at Baltimore/Washington International. We grabbed ourselves new tickets, got on the plane, and headed to sunny, sandy Bermuda.

I don't remember how late we got in, but it was late Friday night. We had been going since the wee hours of the morning, driving to the airport, riding in a cab, traveling through five states by train, and then flying the rest of the way. When John Hughes wrote the script for *Planes, Trains and Automobiles*, he could have been writing about me and my odyssey that day getting to that marathon.

We finally landed in Bermuda, and I had to run this marathon. I had almost no time to rest and recuperate from the trip or recover from my bronchitis.

None of it mattered. I was determined to run the race. I was determined to excel no matter what. The very next morning, I was lined up to race. It was a crowded field and I was there hacking my guts out. People were looking over at me like I had the plague.

None of it mattered.

The starter pistol went off and we all started running. Only twenty-six miles to go. It took a few miles for me to settle down and get into my groove and get running.

I met a few other runners from the United States, from Chicago. One young woman clearly wanted to break away from her group. They were slowing her down, so she decided to lose them.

I joined up with her. She was in shape and obviously a good runner. I wanted to run with her because I knew she'd challenge me, push me to do better.

I'll be honest: Somewhere in the back of my head the little boy in me said I should run with her because I wasn't going to get beaten by a girl. It wasn't going to happen. If she finished, I was going to finish.

We chatted a bit as we ran and ran some more. As the race wore on, the conversation declined. When we got to the twenty-mile marker, we both got less wordy. One of us said, "You okay?" I'm not sure which of us. The response was equally short. "Yeah. You?" "Yeah."

That's it. We kept on running through those last grueling six miles.

We finally finished the marathon—four hours and forty minutes. I stopped and realized something. My lungs were clear. It's like my body under all that stress forced itself to get rid of all the mucus. My hip didn't hurt, either.

I felt like I had just flown to the moon.

I wanted to call my doctor and gloat, but I didn't. I knew I had done the right thing for me, even if it was an example of doing the opposite of what people told me to do. As you will see, this is a core part of my personality and a key to the secret of my success.

After the event, everybody was sitting there with their protein drinks and their Gatorades. They were recharging the way the books and magazines told them.

Then there was me. I was sitting in some Bermuda bar holding a Guinness with a nice froth on top in my right hand. My left hand held a wonderful Cuban cigar already trailing smoke.

I was rehydrating—my way. And I owed myself a treat after reaching my goal. I chose my own path for excellence. It worked. I didn't realize it at the time, but I was becoming a leader in my own right. We'll talk more about the importance of leadership in managing your own money in Chapter 5.

Diligence in Investing

Investing is hard work and requires a lot of patience. Sometimes a stock you think will increase in value takes a long time to do so.

Other times, a holding may go down before it goes up, which requires even more patience.

It doesn't matter whether you do it yourself, have someone do it for you, or work together with an advisor for an approach that's built for you. It's still hard work. The more money you get, the more attention it requires. That means more work.

I've been doing it for years, so obviously I like it. But it's still hard. I'm fond of saying that investing is simple, not easy. "Buy low and sell high" is a remarkably simple concept. Actually doing it well is darn hard.

What many investors end up doing is the exact opposite. They stay out of stocks until the market runs up close to record highs. Then they jump in with both feet. It happened during the 1920s. It happened before the dot-com crash and again before the most recent financial crisis. In the last two cases, media hype got so bad that ordinary people were watching CNBC to monitor their stocks.

> They were all investing through the rearview mirror. Behavioral psychologists call this "hindsight bias." In English, that means that they only feel comfortable investing after the market has done very well—the very definition of buying high.

Often they invest so late in the game that the market falls right around them almost as soon as they get in. The typical investor stays put. They've been taught that way—to ride the highs and lows. After all, the market always comes back . . . eventually.

This even happens in retirement accounts now. In the "old" days, 401(k)s limited changes to every quarter. Investors could only reallocate their investments, not day-trade them. It was a simple, calm, and rational process. I'd meet with employees of corporate clients every quarter to check their results, analyze their investments, and plan for the next quarter as well as for the long term.

Half the time my goal was just preventing them from buying high and selling low—that is, moving out of the funds they were in and into the hot fund from the past quarter. They all wanted to chase success. We'd sit there and discuss it as I tried to argue against pursuing past gains.

Then I'd go back to my office and await the allocation forms only to find a lot of the employees hadn't listened. Too many participants would do the exact opposite of what I had told them. They'd invest and manage through the rearview mirror.

Sadly, while objects in the mirror really are closer than they appear, they are still behind you. Yet investors go on chasing them, falling farther away from their goals in the process.

Maybe it's just pure greed. But when money gets close like that, we lose our heads. We chase it as it slips away. Let me give you an example.

Imagine Cheryl wants to buy into a smoking-hot defense sector mutual fund. At the beginning of the quarter, the fund was trading at $30, but defense stocks are up. In just one quarter, the fund has soared to $35—a 16.67 percent increase.

Cheryl thinks this is a good bet. She looks at the shape of the world and figures defense stocks can't miss. She doesn't have the patience to do the work and analyze which stocks the fund holds and which it might invest in. That's too much work. She trusts her gut and puts all of her $200,000 retirement savings into that one fund. She doesn't even diversify.

Only most of that jump was based on the good news of one company that just signed a new billion-dollar contract. You can't expect it to sign another in the second quarter and another in the third and so on. Instead, maybe it ends up overcommitted and other orders start to slide. By the time the quarter is over, that fund has given back what it just grew and lost a bit as well. Cheryl is already out $30,000.

Hard Work Is Being Diligent

I feel bad for investors like Cheryl. They want investing to be easy. Only it never is. It requires diligence—an intensity of hard work, the kind that many people only muster for things they enjoy.

That means they look for shortcuts—something they saw on the news today, a stock tip from that uncle who spends more time playing computer games than at his job. We all want the get-rich-quick scheme.

That's not investing. Heck, it's not even gambling. As Dave's Tip Number 1 says, it's just throwing your money away.

Investing is a grind. You get up early, check stocks, follow news, watch the wires, study, research, analyze, and do it again day after day.

It reminds me of working out at the gym. It takes patience to get the results you desire.

I know a lot about that world.

Financial Diligence Is a Breeze Compared to This

When I was very young, I always respected people who were bigger, smarter, faster, that sort of thing. People who were clearly exceptional. I remember the landlord from the place we rented right after my father died. His name was Bernie Gordon. He used to lift weights. He was a pretty big man who looked like someone you didn't want to mess with.

Someone like that was easy to look up to as a young boy. I respected him and his dedication. I wanted to lift weights just like him. My mom could tell how important it was to me.

As always, my mom was a huge help. At the house, she would spot me when I was lifting heavy weights. That went on for a couple of years, and I began to put on weight and get some muscles. I was just an early teen and still growing and I was lifting 120 pounds, and that was a lot. One day, it was almost too much.

I had the full 120 pounds on bench pressing and Mom said something funny; I've forgotten what it was, but I started cracking up. My laughter made her start laughing. I've got the weight on my chest and I'm laughing and she's laughing. We were barely able to contain ourselves to get the weights back up on the rack.

When we finally stopped laughing, Mom got a serious look on her face. That's when she stared down at me and in a somber tone said, "It's time for you to join a gym. I'm not strong enough to do this."

I was almost a freshman by this time and a lot of the kids went to the gym. I started working out for real.

I said to myself, "If I'm going to do this, I'm going to be the best at it." I wanted to be a national champion. I meant it, too.

When I was sixteen, I went to my first competition. I really shouldn't have. I wasn't ready. Everyone told me not to go because it's bad to compete and get crushed right off the bat. Thankfully, I don't listen too well when people tell me I can't.

Surprisingly, I did pretty well. Out of all the teenagers in my class, I placed sixth out of thirteen. That was good for a sixteen-year-old. Most people in that range were eighteen or nineteen. Everyone seemed impressed. Everyone but me—and though she'd never admit it, probably my mom, too. She knew I wanted to win, so that's what she wanted for me.

I wanted to be better. That meant hard work.

Lots of hard work. Go to school, then go to the gym and work out. I was building muscle and learning what worked best for my body. I was growing up and growing into one of those Arnold-esque figures. No, that's not ego, that's reality (though my figure looks nothing like that now).

My strategy worked. By the time I was nineteen, I was ready not just to compete. I was ready to win. Win I did, too.

I went nuts competing and won every contest I was in. I'd win the teenage overall division, and then I'd enter the men's division and win my class. Here I was going up against men who were twenty-five to thirty years old who had been competing since their teens.

And I was beating them. Consistently.

They didn't like it, but they respected it. They had to because I kept beating them. The more ticked off at me they were, the harder I worked. Day after day. Lifting, building, becoming ripped. And sweating. Lots of sweating.

By 1985, I was ready for the teenage nationals. More than ready, because I won the heavyweight class. Mr. Connecticut and Mr. America were on the same day. I had a choice to make—do I enter the teenage Mr. Connecticut competition where I was a shoo-in, or do I stretch my comfort zone and enter the nationals against much stiffer competition? Everybody thought I should stay in my state competition so I could win. I chose to go national and face the toughest competition out there. (This was one of my first life lessons about being fearless. In Chapter 7 we discuss fearlessness as one of the core values essential to successful investing.)

I won! National champion. Kids today all get a trophy just for showing up. In my era, you had to work hard just to compete. Winning was an accomplishment that you kept with you long after the trophy was tarnished.

I had previously decided to leave the sport after the nationals. I knew that bodybuilding was not my career choice, but I had the patience to see it through and reach my goal. That's the way to go out. Go out on top—retiring a champion.

The same is true of your money. Even if you weren't planning on retiring until 2010 or 2020, getting out of the stock market in 1999 might still have been a great idea. Getting out on top is always a good thing.

Champions Keep at It

Work works.

The more you do of it, the better things seem. A baseball player who only practices hitting a few balls a day will never be any good. A star who gets up early and swings the bat till his hands are sore will get better. Maybe he won't ever be Ty Cobb or Babe Ruth. But 90 percent of life isn't just showing up. It's doing the work.

That's how we all get good.

The only problem with that is we all want shortcuts. We all want to be rich. Who doesn't? Who doesn't want the house on the water with a big boat parked outside? Who doesn't want the nice car and the ability to travel around the world?

We can all get those things if we're willing to work hard enough. I know. I have those things and getting them wasn't easy.

I got them just like I got the bodybuilding championship. I wanted it, wanted to win. But then I put in the hours. I put in the sweat and tears. I endured the pain.

It came from a belief system my mom instilled in me: that I could accomplish whatever I want. There's nothing special about believing that, even in this day and age. But believing in it is one thing. Doing it is another.

Mom taught me never to give up. Once I started a thing, I had to stick with it till the end.

That's diligence. Sticking to something, day in and day out. That's a characteristic you need in investing. If you don't have it, you have to find someone who does.

When we look again at my example investor, Cheryl, who put all of her $200,000 retirement savings into one mutual fund, I feel sorry for her. Cheryl is probably a nice lady. But she's too busy or too untrained to know what she should be doing with her savings. Instead of doing something smart, she does what she feels she's supposed to do—invest in the stock market.

Every single fiber of our society encourages it. Cheryl simply bought into it. At the wrong time, in the wrong way. And it cost her.

If I could talk to Cheryl like I'm talking to you, I'd tell her that she needs to find an advisor who could protect her from that world. An advisor who can give her the kind of financial portfolio that won't have the major ups and downs that give most investors heartache. I'd tell her that one of the things she needs that advisor to have is a strong work ethic that includes hard work and diligence because that advisor is working for her.

DAVE'S TIP NUMBER 3:
If You Want Something Done, Stick to It

Farmers know all about being diligent. They get up at 4 a.m. or even earlier. They milk cows, feed the livestock, and get ready for a long day working the fields, making sure fences are tended and crops are planted and cared. There are a thousand chores that they need to handle every day. Neglecting any one of those can mean a crop fails and their business fails right along with it. It used to be that most Americans were raised on the farm. That made us an incredibly diligent, persistent, and strong people.

Farmers have the kind of stick-to-itiveness that makes them an American ideal. It's the kind of diligence that might have helped them catch the missing word in the previous paragraph. Don't worry, you probably read right past it. And you're now skimming wondering what you missed. (Hint: There's something missing right after *cared*.)

The world won't end because I deliberately left out the word "for." But suppose that had been a column of figures and I simply left out one number? Picture your tax bill when the IRS reminds you that there was an extra $30,000 you earned last year.

Oops.

Yes, numbers matter. But so does putting them in the right place or even remembering they exist. Let's face it. Americans aren't inherently lazy. But we're comfortable, and that might be more dangerous. Lazy people might know their failings and adapt. Comfortable people just don't worry about their failings. And they can get smacked, like being hit in the face with a fish.

It's a rude awakening. So, I have other questions for you. But I need you to be honest. Remember, it's just us.

1. Do you stick to your resolutions? This year, did you do whatever you promised to yourself or the world that you would do in 2016? (Making a resolution is easy. Keeping it is hard. If it's major—like losing a bunch of weight or learning a new language—those promises take commitment. They require a strategy, and every day you have to keep at them.)

2. Do you always insist on getting the important stuff done before you do anything enjoyable? (This is important because investing is not always enjoyable, but must be a priority.)

3. Be honest with yourself: Are you the type of person who persists in the face of adversity, or have there been times when you have become discouraged and quit? (Remember, it's easy to become discouraged when you watch your portfolio drop in value.)

4. Did you go through a stage in 2008 when you procrastinated opening your investment statements for fear of what was inside? (That's a symptom of discouragement.)

That's diligence. Sticking to something, day in and day out. That's a characteristic you need in investing. If you don't have it, you have to find someone who does .

If you are diligent and are willing to commit the time to manage your own finances, even in retirement, then *maybe* you are able to do so. I said *maybe* because having the time and committing to do it is great, but useless without the aptitude.

If you aren't diligent or you don't have the time—or if answering some of the questions I've posed seems tedious—then you already have an answer. Do-it-yourself doesn't work for you. That means you need someone else—one of the other 7.3 billion people on earth—to handle your finances. Call it "do-it-someone-else."

Ask these interview questions of that "someone else":

1. "How many hours a day are you typically in the office, and how many days a week do you work?"
2. "How is your time divided between client meetings, research, and other tasks?" (If you can get financial advisors talking about their business, there is no telling what you may learn—both good and bad.)
3. "Does anyone else in your organization do research besides you or on your behalf?"
4. "Tell me about some success that you attribute first and foremost to being diligent."
5. "Has your approach to your work or business changed since 2008? If so, how? And if not, why not?" (You need to listen for several indicators here. First, if the advisor had a stock or mutual fund model and is still doing that, that might be described as the definition of insanity—doing things the same way and expecting a different result. Diligence is not just working hard; it's being committed to working smart.)

Please pick the right someone else—an advisor who can stick to it when you can't.

4

FINANCIAL COACHABILITY

Not Your Typical Fish Story

You see, offshore or big-game fishing is a stealth team sport. Everybody has a role and if you do it right, you kick butt. It's given me a chance to be coached and even coach—and to see once again how important it is to be coachable. It's also given me a better perspective on what my role in life is—whether I'm on the deck of our corporate boat, the *Canyon Gear*, or guiding a client through the dangerous waves in the market.

Andrew was a mate on the boat as well as top salesman at my fishing lure company, Canyon Gear. Our slow season for selling fishing lures is November. So he asked me if he could take some time off and crew on a charter fishing boat down at the Great Barrier Reef to fish for giant black marlin. He's from New Zealand and he's fished the reef for six seasons and loves it. I couldn't say no so I gave him the two months off.

He asked me to charter the boat for business as he thought Australia might be a great market to sell our lures, I agreed. I called my friend Brian and invited him over for a week so we could go fish the Great Barrier Reef. Brian used to work with us. He and I had a great history together. He went from being a barely successful advisor to top in his field. I really helped him and he was coachable.

Our destination, the Great Barrier Reef, is one of those amazing wonders of nature that most of us only see on the National Geographic Channel. Located off the northeast coast of Australia, it's 1,400 miles long.

Giant black marlin were the reason for the trip.

For a sports fisherman, the black marlin is like a hole in one in golf. They are enormous fish—weighing in at 1,000 pounds and more.

Brian and I arrived in Australia and went directly to the boat. The sixty-foot, Aussie-built and custom Sport Fisherman left shore and anchored overnight inside the reef. This was going to be our routine for the next five nights, being at anchor and never touching land. I felt right at home; I've always enjoyed sleeping on board, especially at anchor. The next morning we got up and the captain had our day all planned out for us.

We fished for a couple hours, working up a sweat under the hot southern sun, filling the coolers with several baitfish. Even catching those was fun. You start off your day with a healthy sense of accomplishment. We earned a break. The captain anchored on the reef for snorkeling and a chance to cool off.

That was our chance to go swimming . . . with the sharks.

Now there were sharks all around us; we're talking up to twenty feet long, with big teeth, just like we've seen portrayed in cartoons. They don't usually mess with humans, but it pays to be wary. It's like being at SeaWorld only you're in the tank. When we finished snorkeling, we went back to the boat to have lunch, feeling completely refreshed. Then we took the boat offshore to start trolling for black marlin.

The plan was that Brian and I would take turns fishing from the fighting chair, trying to grab ourselves the prize. Brian had never gone deep-sea fishing before, where he had to fight from the chair. And I had him out there trying to catch the biggest marlin in the world, the black marlin, but I wasn't worried because I knew he was coachable.

There's something you need to understand when you're offshore or big-game fishing. You're wearing a harness that is attached to the rod, you're clipped in, but you aren't strapped into the chair. It's a little precarious when you first do it. If you aren't careful, the situation can go wrong. Badly wrong.

If the fish launches and goes away fast and your rod hits the gunwale, you can get pulled overboard by the fish. There you are being dragged through the water by a massive marlin—every fisherman's worst nightmare.

Fishing for black marlin is serious deep-sea fishing. It's you against the fish—man against nature.

It can take an hour of fighting to bring in a fish this size. It's backbreaking exercise. You're exhausted; your arms are tired and your legs are burning from working the fish. It takes all you've got. Then sometimes it takes even more.

If everything goes right, you reel in your 130-pound line; you come down and try to get a crank, to bring him closer. You can tell he's getting somewhat close because the color of the line changes. It helps you measure distance or depth.

You can feel your heart beat faster. You're finally close to this fight being over, and then the little bugger decides he's going to go on a run and takes off again.

So all that line that you just worked to get back on the reel is gone; it's pulling off and out again.

That was the battle Brian and I were there for.

I took the first fish. I wanted to teach him how, because he had never caught a fish out of the chair. The first fish came in, and in five minutes I had it to the boat. It was a nice fish, 400 pounds, but not the prize; plus, it was easier for me, because I had experience. I doubt he learned much in those few minutes.

Then it was his turn. He hooked the second fish, and the line started spooling out very fast. Then we saw it jump out of the water. The fish looked like a school bus flying through the air.

We had hit the mother lode.

Andrew and I looked at each other thinking, "Oh crap, we're going to be here for a while," since Brian had never fought a fish from the chair. The line was 130-pound test. Brian's scrawny 170-pound butt was sitting in this fighting chair, and every time the fish ran, Brian was thinking that he would be pulled overboard.

He was holding on for dear life. He wouldn't reel the fish in because of fear. Instead he kept holding on to the chair, white-knuckling it. He was afraid if he let go, he would get pulled in. Who could blame him for reacting that way? This wasn't a game. This was real life. But you have to let go of the chair to fight the fish.

I was watching him, observing how he handled it. And I realized he needed my help. He needed a coach to help him through it. I had been his business mentor for years and he proved to be coachable. I just had to do it again, this time with a huge black marlin along for the ride. Brian needed someone to help him coordinate. It's a lot like what I do in the office. Not just for him, but for my clients. I try to help them in troubled seas and keep them from going under.

Now I was going to be his fishing mentor. I said, "Brian, listen to me. I'm going to hold you, you're not going anywhere. You have to fight the fish. Trust me. Do you trust me?"

I grabbed his harness and pulled it back and got him firmly in the fighting chair.

"Trust me, do what I say."

He didn't say anything. He just started doing what I told him. He started fighting the fish and believing in himself. Believing in the team. I held on to his harness for fifty minutes so that he would have the confidence to continue fighting the fish. My arm was so sore from holding him back. As the fish was pulling, I was coaching Brian. I was doing what Andrew had once done with me.

It was a fight that neither one of us will ever forget. He'd reel that sucker in and it would jump into the air, trying to shake free of the hook. Then it would speed away, diving; again and again this repeated. Brian was wearing out, but he kept on fighting. I was wearing out, but I wouldn't let him down and he knew that.

Finally, you could see the change in the line. Our black marlin was getting close enough to get a good look. Close enough for Brian to see his victory.

He finally landed his fish about fifty minutes after we began. It wasn't an ordinary catch. It was big. Huge. A 900-plus pounder. A big black marlin that we landed together.

We let it go.

Offshore or big-game fishing is about the hunt. We didn't need a trophy. The trophy we had was in our hearts and our memories. We wanted that majestic marlin to challenge fishermen for years to come.

In the Chair Alone?

Life is more than just a fish story.

I've been involved in big-game fishing ever since I decided to pursue a business venture and buy that fishing lure company. Every time I went fishing, I'd try out new gear and learn from fellow fishermen what they wanted or needed. Getting into a new venture required that I be coachable. One of the key things I learned was that every fisherman needs to think like a crew member, not an individual. I had to stretch my comfort zone and go from being a lone sportsman to being a team member. Brian and I succeeded as a team. We had a fantastic captain. We had a great first mate. We had a good crew who knew their jobs. Brian proved to be as diligent and coachable an angler as he was a financial advisor; that's part of what makes him such a great advisor. When it comes to our financial health, many of us try to go it alone. We're like Brian, sitting in that chair on our own, waiting to be pulled overboard or holding on for dear life so that we aren't. Even when we ask for help, we often do it scattershot. We'll grab some advice from a CPA, some guidance from an insurance agent. We don't seek out the best coach, perhaps because we are afraid to be coached.

To have a winning team one needs to be willing to learn and be coachable.

Look at the last decade in your financial life. We've gone from a good economy to a stock market collapse that investors now call the "panic of 2008." And then back again—for now.

Think back for a second and try to remember how terrifying that was to everyone. The S&P 500 peaked at 1,565 on October 9, 2007. By March 9, 2009, it had pancaked to 676, less than half where it had been at its peak.

Companies closed. Careers were lost. And if you had a decent amount in the stock market, you lost money for retirement or to pay for your kids' college.

You might have even pulled out of the market sometime in the early stages of that crash, before losing 40 to 60 percent of everything you had. If you did, good for you. But you were probably also slow to get back in, skittish about a crazy market that no one seems to understand.

The whole time, you were alone in the fighting chair. Trying to reel in a big fish. But you also had to captain the boat. And be the first mate. And crew the rest of the vessel. Nobody was helping you because you didn't have the right coaching.

The reality is, you can't control what the market does. No one can. Some bad news comes out and people panic and sell. You can't control that. You could have done the best research and picked the best company, but if somebody else did something crazy, you lost.

All the knowledge in the world won't help you if you don't know what to do with it.

My purpose is to help you fix that.

How I Grew into Being a Coach

Turning a group of employees into a team is hard for entrepreneurs to learn. It's the natural evolution of leadership, but also requires the leader to be coachable. You can demand a lot from your players, but when you turn your back, they have to be coachable also and willing to work as a team.

That was a hard transition for me: I had to go from being the coachable one to the one who coaches. I told my managers that each one of them was jointly and severally liable for understanding what we wanted to accomplish. If they didn't get it, they needed to figure it out from each other or find an answer by being coachable in a proactive way.

And if I didn't hear from them that they didn't fully understand it, I assumed that everyone understood it, and it was on them if something didn't get done properly or according to schedule. As they were trained, they became responsible for making things work on their own. It was up to them to communicate and pull together. I taught that, but it took time for some people to learn it.

Every department needed that type of coaching because I didn't have a team. I had a bunch of individual players. I needed some-one to elevate some skills. Someone had to take my challenge and become great.

I got very frustrated. And I find sometimes when you get frus-trated like that, you make changes. I had read the books. I had learned the books. But I got frustrated because I needed to put my own stamp on things.

So I realized that the skill set that got me to where I had gotten by age 45 had to change. I had to be more of a team coach than just the person who did everything; but I, too, needed a coach in order to take the next step of my business growth.

That inspired me to make changes and to finally turn our growing business into a winning team. I set out looking for various department heads. I had a few people who didn't work out, but that's inevitable as you convert from running a business to leading a team.

When I hired people initially, I had some misfires. Every manager does. There's a learning curve when you try to go from being that alpha male entrepreneur to becoming a business owner—part leader, part coach of a team.

When you try to make that transition, you're going to make some mistakes.

Hiring a couple of employees was fine. Where it became a challenge in my life was trying to build a real team. Eventually, I decided I needed to focus on it. I hired a business coach to help me; I was ready to be coachable. He helped me realize that I needed to launch a concerted effort to promote or hire people in all parts of our company who were better than me in their respective departments—because I was running at capacity. We'd have meetings and there would be fifteen people sitting there and we'd agree that "we've got to do this." Then everyone would turn to me and pass the buck right back to me. "Well, Dave, you're the best one at that."

Finding the Right Coach for Our Corporate Fishing Team

The best way for any fishing lure manufacturer to sell more lures is to enter and actually win fishing tournaments. Fishermen are like golfers. If you tell a golfer that a particular set of new clubs will shave three strokes off his score, he will pay whatever price for them. If a fishing boat wins a tournament using a certain type of lure, every big-game fisherman suddenly has to have that lure in his tackle box.

I decided to embrace the New York Yankees' philosophy and went out to get the best coach I could. I decided to hire a ringer. My team entered a tournament called the Mid-Atlantic 500 tournament. It's a big, important tournament with hundreds of boats. For fishermen, it's a big deal.

Deep-sea fishing is a pretty small world. I got to know a lot of the top talent through my lure company. I was always on the lookout for new ideas, new concepts, and maybe even a star to advertise a product. Canyon Gear gave me a good view of that world.

The best people get a good word-of-mouth reputation. I decided to hire a captain I'll call "Bob." Bob is known as one of the best captains in the world for good reason. He is top, top echelon.

Our salesman Andrew knew him. I remember thinking, "Okay, I've got the ringer, let's go." I felt so smug. I was sure we would do great in the tournament.

Make Sure You Have the Right Coach for the Job

Boy, was I wrong. We did terrible. We had a great captain, but we didn't have the right captain for this application. Bob was and is a great captain when it comes to fishing the Pacific. And that was where most of his experience came from.

But the kind of fishing we were doing right there wasn't necessarily his niche. I had transferred a star halfway across the world into waters he didn't know—to a team he didn't know—and I expected us to win. I might as well have thrown an extra anchor or two out there when the boat was moving, just to slow us up even more.

That was it for tournaments that year. But many lessons were learned. Successful people are supposed to try new things. But you also have to learn not to make the same mistakes twice. I had a good idea and poor execution.

My Second Attempt at Finding the Right Fishing Coach

I decided I was going to go on a trip to market our lures in the Dominican Republic and St. Thomas, where there are many American fishermen during the season. There was no question: I was going to hire another ringer. Live and learn. So this time I hired a captain who knew these areas, who fished them full-time.

I hired the best captain I could find—a man named Jim. Jim has fished the Dominican Republic and St. Thomas every year. He's one of the absolute best. Talk to captains, anyone on the dock, and he's the man.

I told him, "I want you to build a fishing team, a good team. I know it takes time, it takes money." The goal was for him to go out and find the best people. As a coach, I was hoping he'd be a good manager.

Jim was to go hire a really good first mate. After that, he was supposed to find other good anglers who could come into tournaments with us. The goal was simple: Build a good corporate fishing team and then practice together to win.

It wasn't to be.

Jim ran a charter boat for many years. There's nothing wrong with that. He was, as I said, a great charter captain.

The problem was that Jim was used to being the alpha dog in his world, and the boat was his world.

Unfortunately, Canyon Gear had to be run like a business because it was a business. I knew what I wanted, too, and I wanted to help elevate him as a manager. I said, "You're a great fisherman, Jim, go build a team." In retrospect, he didn't try to build a team because he was not coachable.

It's hard to coach people you don't see every day. Managing the boat, as part of Canyon Gear, while still running my company was a ton of extra work. One day, I was riding to the airport, on the way to England, chatting with Jim on the phone the whole time. For two solid hours, I tried to coach him with management guidance and advice. I wanted to inspire him to be a better leader, a better team builder, a better coach of the team.

I was hoping I could lean on him and that he could stretch his comfort zone.

The reality of it was that Jim didn't want to stretch his comfort zone or learn to be coachable.

We went into a couple of tournaments with a ragtag team—whoever Jim could grab. They didn't have the best skills or even a desire to win. We just grabbed one guy from here, another from there. We couldn't win anything. Our poor team results certainly didn't help us sell more lures.

Jim really didn't have the experience of building the team, and I foolishly tried to make him do it anyhow.

Now I learned another lesson. I had hired a star player to be a manager and he just didn't want to learn.

Be Coachable

One of the biggest challenges for every business is finding coachable team members and finding the right coach. Building and managing a team is the natural evolution of a good leader.

That doesn't happen overnight. Pro sports teams churn talent on a regular basis. A good NFL team drafts new players fresh out of school, signs big-name free agents, and is constantly scouting for coachable talent everyone missed. The only way to turn that group of players into a team is with the right coach, but only if the players are coachable.

It wasn't my natural modus operandi. I'm used to being a one-man team. Growing the business has forced me to change. Now it's actually the most fun, exciting part of expanding the businesses I own—building the teams that run them—whether they are giving financial advice or helping people enjoy their free time by fishing.

Most people would agree that LeBron James is one of the best basketball players to ever play the game. Many with that level of talent would be filled with arrogance and eventually become uncoachable. LeBron is the opposite. Years ago, he was humble enough to know that his skills on the basketball court didn't necessarily translate to investing. He decided he wanted a mentor and was determined to hire the best. As a result, it's widely known that Warren Buffett is his financial mentor. You'd be hard pressed to find a better mentor. Luckily, most of *my* clients don't have access to Warren Buffett, so they have to settle for me!

The Wrong Coaching Can Be Hazardous to Your Health

There is one way Wall Street sells investing—greed. It's easier and allows major financial businesses to promote stocks going up, which keeps people in the markets. Other advisors try the fear angle.

There are some logical points for both strategies. People invest in stocks to make money. That doesn't make them greedy. It makes them prudent.

And just because we live in the greatest nation in history doesn't mean bad times don't happen. We've endured foreign invasion, two world wars, a civil war, and enough economic downturns to make the biggest market bull fidgety.

Whether you are bombarded with greed or fear depends on what the market is doing at the time. As P/Es go up and the market booms, unscrupulous brokers will keep pushing market optimism. They'll urge everyone, no matter their means, to throw cash into the markets.

They are like carnival barkers calling on people to hop on the roller coaster of disaster. Sure, the coaster feels good as it starts uphill in a slow, steady climb. Then it speeds up—faster and faster around curves. Everyone on the ride is having a wonderful time, adrenaline pumping through their veins.

Then it plummets.

Suddenly. Violently.

The market starts dropping. Economist Nouriel Roubini starts appearing on every TV network that can find him. Roubini is famously known as Dr. Doom in investment circles. He's also called a "permabear" and journalists love to trot him out when they have switched from hyping the upside and become obsessed with hyping the downturn.

As the market drops, we lose some or maybe all of what we made during that mad roller-coaster ride earlier. It's fun on the way up, exciting, in fact. But on the way down it's often terrifying. The longer the ride up takes, the longer you can expect things to go plummeting downward. And as the coaster is hurtling downward, you are holding on for dear life.

Most people spend their entire lives caught in that endless ride—on the way up, on the way down, and the terrifying crash as the ride comes to an abrupt halt.

I used to be just as involved in it as you may be. More so, because that's how I made my living.

Seeking a Coach for My Financial Company

I've explained what made me think the dot-com collapse of 2000 was happening before it did happen. But finding a good solution was harder than you might think.

I had a small operation at the time, not the 100-plus-member team that I have now. This was twelve years into my career, and my group only had one full-timer. That's it. I looked at the markets and thought, based on market history, that we were heading into a downturn sooner rather than later.

The year was 1999, and unlike the singer Prince, I wasn't ready to party. I sat down with my one assistant to have a serious talk. I explained our dilemma. We had to get these clients out of the market. We had to move them into more conservative portfolios.

I was worried that if I moved them into investments that were simple and had low fees, I might not even be able to pay my assistant. But my clients always come first.

She and I had to work together to pull it off. I thought that I could get her mind working, focusing on the problem at hand. I needed her active support, but I needed the unconscious part of her mind looking at the problem as well. That's often referred to as the *reticular activating system*. It's the part of the brain programmed to notice opportunities when your goals are powerful. Remaining employed was a powerful motivator for both of us.

When you go out and buy a black Cadillac, the reticular activating system is the part of your mind that lets you see twenty of them on the street the next day. You never saw twenty black Cadillacs in a month before, but now your unconscious mind is programmed to see them.

My assistant Suzanne had her reticular activating system looking around for opportunities, firing on all cylinders. She was also an excellent call screener, the gatekeeper to my corporate castle. Every salesperson who would call in would get shut down. Sometimes I'd hear her from my office: "No, no. You're not getting through to him. He's very busy." She knew the people I needed to talk to and never let anyone waste my time.

When a Student Is Ready, the Teacher Appears

Finally, an unusual call came in. The office at the other end of the line held one of the most important people ever to come into my life—Rick, the man who went on to become my mentor and my coach every day until his tragic death in a boating accident.

Rick's company was talking about using more conservative investment opportunities for clients that might address my market concerns. I might not have to close my office in the midst of an upcoming market collapse.

Suzanne listened to the call and instead of tossing the message into the trash, she passed it on to me. She walked into my office and handed me a note with contact information on it. "Dave, I don't usually send sales calls to you, but you should talk to these guys," she said with a smile. "They seem pretty good. Number one, the guy works as a mentor and he's doing about five times the volume you are doing, and number two, he has these strategies that are more conservative financial tools and might be what you're looking for."

I was truly impressed. Because I had sat her down and focused her on the direction we were aiming for, she took a call that she wouldn't normally have taken. And though she was still my gatekeeper, she listened closely. She didn't tell them that I didn't take calls from salespeople. She didn't hang up. Instead, she listened a minute longer and provided us with an opportunity.

The financial future of my clients, even my own future, turned—just from that one phone call.

I flew out to San Diego to learn more.

Rick had filled his conference room with financial advisors. I was in my thirties then and remember there were some older guys there. I don't know how old they were. They were probably in their fifties, which now doesn't seem so old.

Rick was forty-two at the time, and he had his signature buzz-cut hairdo, all spiked up top. He was quite successful, earning $2 million a year in revenue from his financial practice that focused on conservative strategies. That meant he was handling several times that number in assets. I was impressed. But when he started talking to us, he came across to some as unsophisticated because of his folksy way.

He told us his story. He had been a successful builder until the real estate sector hit some tough times. So he studied to become a financial advisor and found his true calling. The skills he learned from marketing real estate were transferable. In fact, that background made him even better.

He seemed to understand the essence of what we did as financial advisors. A good advisor is the coach. His (or her) job is to guide investors through the decision-making process. He should educate the clients so they can make their own investment decisions, and keep coaching them to make the right choices.

Rick started explaining his operation. He was mentoring advisors, but his real business was marketing his financial practice. I sat there watching and listening. It sounded like I could do what was right for my clients and still keep my office open.

I was hooked. Many of the others in the audience weren't as pleased. These stuffy financial advisor types with thirty-five years in the business all wanted to bash Rick for his style. He left the room and I could hear them whining, "Well, my style is different." A couple of them kept going back and forth about it, tearing Rick down.

At that time, I didn't know Rick as I later would. I had just met him, just like the others had. But I was tired of their complaints. We didn't just come to San Diego to learn. We came to help our clients. And they wanted to criticize him because of his simple style and a haircut they didn't like.

Finally, I stood up and got their attention. I said, "Let me say something." One by one, I stared down the complainers. Then I asked them, "Do you make $2 million a year? Do you make $2 million?"

You could have heard a pin drop.

I kept going. "You know why Rick makes $2 million? Because he helps more people than any one of us." I let that sink in for a second. Then I underlined it. "That's why he's paid more. Because he helps more people. So I've got news for all of you," I said, addressing each of the whiners in turn: "Compared to him, you don't have a style, and you don't have a style, and you don't have a style."

Then I addressed the group again. I was in full sales mode because I was so angry. "If your ego is going to be this damn big that you're not willing to be coachable, you should have stayed wherever you came from and not come out here to San Diego." I looked at the group one more time and added, "I may not be exactly like him, but I can learn from him."

From that day on, Rick had me hooked. I realized I defended him not because of his style but because of his substance. Rick took me under his wing and coached me to coach others.

We were placing together some business through his firm, like my advisors are doing now through Advisors' Academy and Sound Income Strategies, our registered investment advisory firm. Because I did well right off the bat, he helped me out. He'd fly me out to San Diego and for two days I'd sit with him the whole time—in every client meeting and everything he did.

I'd pick his brain in between. I learned a lot from him. Occasionally, if I had an issue, I'd call him up on the phone and ask him questions.

How I Went from a Player to Coach

Rick and I worked closely, and I grew a lot in what I was doing. I saw it. Rick saw it. And my clients saw it.

I was thinking a great deal about becoming a better communicator. I wanted to take my complex client-facing educational process and make it simple so that I could motivate people to take action. You can be the smartest advisor in the world, but if you can't motivate people to take action by talking their language, you're not helping.

That's the essence of being a financial advisor. Our goal is always to help people. An important part of the coaching role is that you have to learn to mentor.

I spent the years until Rick's untimely death learning how to get better at educating clients. After I recovered from the shock of his loss, I was inspired to put my thoughts in writing. That brain dump got me to better understand why I was doing what I was doing.

I had it in my head but wanted to turn it into a step-by-step process. Some of it was intuitive. Most of it came when I started to better observe how clients reacted to my explanations.

I knew what worked, so I did it. When I started to break down why it worked, I understood the *why*. I was able to put it into a process so I could teach others. I learned that I'm something of a natural teacher. Even more, I like to teach.

I never expected to lose my mentor so soon, but I was fortunate that I was as coachable as I could possibly be while I had him in my life. Rick had done so much mentoring and coaching that I wanted to emulate him. So that was what I decided to do. It was about helping others become better communicators. I wanted to make sure it was something other people could learn from.

That's when I went to the number two man who was now running Rick's company. I had something to prove to myself. I offered to teach some of the other advisors. I even told him to give me a cross section of people, to see what I could do with various skill sets.

I wasn't doing it for the money. I wanted to see if my brain dump worked. If I had learned enough not just to do, but to teach. I wanted to test and to see if what I had figured out and put on paper was transferable to others. I offered to mentor them through training. The company paid me a few dollars for the work. But the work was its own reward.

I coached for about a year and a half, from 2004 to 2005. Out of roughly a thousand advisors, they gave me twenty-six with a wide range of talents and skills. After only a year, seventeen of the twenty-six had made a quantum leap in their performance.

That's like coaching a minor league ball club and sending two-thirds of them to the big leagues the following season.

I had my eureka moment. I had just proved that my process of teaching others was transferable. It made me do a life check. It was 2005 and I was turning forty. At that point I realized children probably weren't in the cards for me. I was working three or four days a week and had plenty of money to do what I wanted. I had a boat docked nearby. I was taking three-day weekends and doing what I wanted.

Yet something was missing. I asked myself, "What's going to be my legacy? What will people remember me by?" I could picture it: *Here lies David J. Scranton, successful entrepreneur, lived the good life, now he's dead.*

Was that really what work's all about? I knew the answer before I asked. No. Emphatically, no. I had developed a set of skills I wanted to teach others so that they could pursue their dreams and could also help others in turn.

That's when I branched off and started Advisors' Academy in the end of 2006.

Now I do both of my work passions. I help others with their money and I teach financial advisors from around the nation to do it as well.

Finding Yourself a Good Coach

I'm not going to pretend I'm Mother Teresa. Hardly anyone is that selfless. I like the challenge of work. I like winning by helping my clients succeed. And yes, I don't know anyone who doesn't like a good payday.

All that goes out the window when you are helping people. I've helped thousands of people in my career. That number has grown geometrically since I started Advisors' Academy. Now all of the founding members of the company are able to help mentor and coach other advisors, and they, in turn, help thousands of clients as well.

On some level, I think I've always been somewhat of a mentor. I've always been the one refining how things were done and then sharing my results with others.

That sentiment grew when I met Rick. He was like a mentor on steroids. The man was everywhere. If the advisors needed a hand, Rick always found the time.

I understand how he felt. Helping my team, watching them grow, coaching them is heartwarming. Maybe it's a proxy for not having children, but I think every one of us enjoys helping others.

It's an essential skill not just with advisors but with clients. I look for coachable players. Most of the people I help have some financial knowledge. Sometimes I have to teach them. Other times I have to *un*teach them and get them to give up bad money habits, such as spending too much and desperately following where the markets have already gone.

That doesn't just mean teaching. It means guidance. They don't call us financial *advisors* for nothing. We don't make the final decisions. We help our clients make the right ones. That takes time, patience, and the ability to build a rapport.

A great coach can't play the game: He can only get the most out of the players if they are coachable. The investor is one of the players. Investors are the ones who make the decisions, either themselves or through an advisor. But either way, investors are making the decision and need to be coachable.

That investor also needs to find the right coach for the tournament. Don't do what I did in the story of my corporate fishing team. If your money is in the stock market, then find that captain who specializes in the stock market. Conversely, if your money is in the universe of non-stock income-generating alternatives, then find a captain with that strategy as well.

A good advisor is the coach. The advisor's job is to guide investors, the clients, through the decision-making process. The advisor should educate clients so they can make their own investment decisions.

But a financial advisor needs a coach as well. I'm proud to say much of my coaching knowledge came from Rick—things he taught me and even the way he taught me. That first day of training helped me realize that I didn't want to be like those guys stuck in their way. I wanted to be coachable. That day, I decided on my new business model: to be the advisor who focused on everything other than the stock market. I wanted to specialize in the universe of non-stock income-generating strategies.

Some of how I advise people comes from my mom, who always had time to help me learn. Now she's with me when I help others. The rest comes from Rick. They were my two best coaches. If you seek out an advisor, you need someone who will fill that coaching role for you but remain coachable himself.

DAVE'S TIP NUMBER 4:
Find a Coach and Be Coachable—
or Learn How to Coach Yourself

If you want to learn about coaching, you also need to learn about being coachable. It's not a one-way street. Sure, broadcasters call coaches generals on the field. But most don't have that kind of authority. They might bench a bad player. And if it's a high-priced player, maybe they can't even do that.

Coaches are motivators, planners, strategists. But they can't do anything unless the people they coach allow themselves to be coached.

The best example I've ever seen is in the movie *Rocky*. It's a Sylvester Stallone masterpiece of both writing and acting, but what resonates with me is what it teaches about coaching and being coachable.

Early on, we see how trainer Mickey is disgusted with Rocky, not because he is a bad fighter but because he is wasting what God gave him. There's a confrontation in the gym, and Rocky demands to know why Mickey is always so mean to him. Right there in front of everybody, as all eyes turn toward the pair, Mickey tells Rocky: "Because you had the talent to become a good fighter! And instead of that, you became a leg-breaker to some cheap, second-rate loan shark!"

It sets up Mickey as an expert, but also as a moral authority. Later, when Rocky gets his big chance, Mickey asks, then begs, to train him. That sets off Rocky, who is angry at being ignored all these years. But after a brief rant, Rocky runs after Mickey. We see the pair settle their differences from a distance, without any dialogue. At the end, they shake hands. Partners.

That's what coaching needs to be—a partnership.

I think this resonated with me because so much of the movie takes place in a gym, the same place where I've fought a lot of my battles and won a lot of my victories.

I'm not asking you to get in the ring and take a couple hundred punches from Apollo Creed. If you've been in the market since 2000, you probably already feel worse than Rocky—beaten and battered inside. You've taken everything modern investing can throw at you—two massive market collapses, the rise and fall of pop culture investing, and more.

It's one heck of a punch in the gut just to admit it.

Now you need to step out of the ring, so to speak. You need to be able to set all that aside and ask yourself: Am I willing to learn from all that happened instead of trying to repeat it? Am I willing to ignore what I've been hearing all these years and listen to someone else? Someone new? Saying something that might run contrary to the Wall Street propaganda I've heard my whole life?

Here are a few questions to help with your self-analysis to determine whether your level of "coachability" is sufficient to go it alone:

1. When someone suggests to you that there may be a better way of doing things, do you find yourself getting a bit defensive? (If so, think about what that means about your coachability or lack thereof.)
2. Have you ever read a self-help book or attended a course with the goal of changing the way you do something, but then came home and slid into old habits?
3. Are you secretly somewhat happy when a household repair crops up because you look forward to the challenge of doing it yourself? Or are you fine with calling a professional when you determine it's in your best interest?
4. Do you take guidance and instruction well in your professional life?
5. Do you attribute any part of your personal success in life to a coach or mentor?
6. Would the people closest to you describe you as being set in your ways?

Think back to *Rocky*. Much of the movie is about the training. In fact, the whole *Rocky* franchise does those classic sports training sequences better than any other. Rocky boxing, Rocky doing push-ups, Rocky doing speed training.

You didn't see Rocky constantly griping about what his coach told him to do. No. Instead, Rocky listened. He took in what Mickey told him. He learned. He grew as a boxer. Grew as a man. So did

Mickey. He was no longer just a guy who ran a gym. He was back in his boxing prime with knowledge and experience. Together they made a powerful team.

At the end of the day, Rocky won not only because he had a good coach but because eventually he proved himself to be extremely coachable. The thing about investing is that no one knows it all. A successful investor knows his limitations and when to reach out directly or indirectly for help. If you are the type of person—and gentlemen, I'm talking to you—who would rather drive around for hours than stop and ask for directions, then maybe you need to seek the help of an advisor. Here are some great interview questions:

1. "Who is your mentor in the financial industry, and what have you learned from him or her?" (An advisor who has no mentor might be subconsciously uncoachable).

2. "How many financial books do you read in an average year, other than what is required for CE credits? And what percentage of those affect your thinking and money management style?" (Ideally, you are looking for some-one who reads several books annually; after all, financial advisors need to educate themselves to stay on top of their business. Also, advisors who have not adapted their money management style might not be as coachable as you need them to be. On the other hand, someone who changes management style with virtually every book might not be a leader; see Chapter 5, on leadership.)

3. "Tell me about a time where you changed your approach or way of thinking about something because you discov-ered evidence that compelled you to change."

4. "Tell me about a time in your life, business or otherwise, where being coached by someone allowed you to achieve a higher level of success."

An experienced advisor knows a ton and can help you figure out how to keep the markets from beating you up a third time. The only catch is that even experienced advisors don't know everything. They need to know their limitations and be coachable.

Go on, you can hear the *Rocky* music in your head. I can too. I think you have some steps to climb.

5

FINANCIAL LEADERSHIP

> Many people think that being coachable and being a leader are diametrically opposed opposites, when ideally they go hand in hand.

MERICA HAS BEEN blessed with some great leaders, just as some of its most successful companies have. If your future and that of your children is ultimately in your hands, the question becomes, "Are you a true leader?" That sounds like a simple question, only it's not. We all like to picture ourselves part Patton and part Churchill, JFK, and Reagan. If it's actually true, great; you own perhaps the most scarce of the seven principles that qualify you to bear all the responsibility of a do-it-yourselfer. Otherwise you should strongly consider finding that leader, someone who will question everything on your behalf.

I don't watch a ton of movies, but you can't help but see a few of the best. Look at Tom Hanks in *Saving Private Ryan*. Hanks is an everyman. He's not a huge presence like John Wayne or the "action hero" type like Tom Cruise in *Mission Impossible*.

Yes, Hanks and his men had an impossible mission, finding one man-sized needle in a haystack as big as D-Day. That didn't stop him. He didn't try to pretend the mission made sense; he just bent his will to do the job.

And he did more than that. He led. He showed his men how to triumph through thick and thin. Even when the odds were wildly against his little outfit, he figured out creative ways to win. And he didn't just tell his men to fight. He encouraged them by leading out front.

That's the way wars used to be fought. Generals would lead from the front and often die doing so. Today, generals might sit in comfortable headquarters away from the front lines, but our leaders still lead from the front.

Look at two great presidents—JFK and Reagan. Both did more than just get elected. They led the nation. They challenged it, encouraged it, and demanded its excellence.

When President Kennedy told the crowd at Rice University in 1962 that we were going to go to the moon, he didn't paint a rosy picture. He demanded success: "We choose to go to the moon. We choose to go to the moon in this decade and do the other things, not because they are easy, but because they are hard."

That speech and that command galvanized a nation so that we landed on the moon six years after his untimely death.

When President Reagan gave his address at the Brandenburg Gate in June 1987, he didn't just speak to the American public. He challenged our number one enemy, the Soviet Union. He called on Soviet leader Mikhail Gorbachev to eliminate the Berlin Wall that separated East and West. "Mr. Gorbachev, open this gate! Mr. Gorbachev, tear down this wall!" he demanded.

Two years later, the wall came down.

Leaders Break the Rules and Forge Their Own Path

Financial advisors have tons of rules that we have to follow to the letter. There are reasons those rules exist—to protect clients. And we stick to them like glue. My math side almost enjoys some of those rules because there's a built-in logic to them.

There are other areas where I'm not a rule follower. Where I like to do things my way. That's the entrepreneurial side in me.

But to be a rule breaker you have to learn the rules to know which ones to break and when. I'm talking about the investing rules that are drummed into every financial advisor from day one. There is no regulation behind them. It's more conventional wisdom, and I'm not especially conventional.

I have a pattern that's lasted my whole life. First I learn the rules by rote. I become an expert on the rules. I study the textbooks. I learn from the experts. I read their books. I watch them on TV. I listen to them at conferences. I try to get to know their rules as well as they know them.

Then I try to make those rules my own. I make small tweaks in the way things are done. I won't *always* do it the way it's been done if I think there's a smarter way to do it. I'll mark up the books and try to redo their math. I'll run through scenarios in my head to see if those rules hold up under every type of market and for every type of client.

I try to make the rules better. Better for me. Better for my clients. Better for my team. Better for everyone.

That's what we teach as well. At the Advisors' Academy, the founding members and I want other experts to be learning our approach, knowing what we do and how we help clients. Over time, the stars define their own path and make those rules their own, just as I did. But first they need to do the heavy lifting. They need to learn and be coachable.

You have to be reasonably analytical to do this. You have to dig into your own processes and how you do things. It's what I've practiced. Now it's what I teach.

First I had to learn it myself.

One of my most successful attempts at this strategy came because of what I saw happening in the markets. I had modified my investment model before the tech bubble burst in 2000. I had advised all of my clients to get out of the stock market and started putting them in conservative income-generating investments. Normally, I would have earned less doing it that way. However, because I was in the right place at the right time, I gained more clients and made up for any potential losses. It kept my clients financially healthy and they loved me for it.

As you recall, it was an incredibly tough time in the markets for everyone. Stocks were dropping. People were panicking. The same investors who had tested the market at its highest points were pulling out as it was dropping. Lots of financial advisors couldn't handle the rapid developments. Fortunes were lost. Careers crashed, just like the markets.

Leaders Are Honest with Others as Well as Themselves

In the midst of this chaos, I still had a business to run and I had to be profitable. I had to analyze every aspect of that business to see what was working and what wasn't.

One piece of my business was giving dinner seminars. When I did the math, I realized that I was losing money there. I hadn't realized it before, because most of my current clients knew me and trusted me enough that they were willing to pull most of their money out of the market and invest it in non-stock income-generating strategies. But it was too big of a leap of faith for some new prospects to make after completing eighteen of the best years ever in the stock market. I was doing well enough financially, too, which hid the problem until I crunched the numbers.

And I always crunch the numbers.

I looked in the mirror and was brutally honest with myself. I had to admit that I simply wasn't a good enough salesman.

Saying you can't sell well enough in a client-oriented business is like saying you're a doctor with a poor bedside manner. You know your business after decades of study, but there's something missing. Something essential.

There was only one answer. I knew I had to get better. I had to learn to really sell. To sell better than I ever had. To connect with clients the way I was supposed to.

That was 2001, and I was doing the lead presentation at a Las Vegas financial summer conference because I was one of the top advisors. The audience filled the room. There were several hundred advisors there. I stepped to the podium to give them guidance because I was the No. 2 salesman in the company.

They thought I was a sales superhero. If I had gone up onstage wearing a big S on my chest and a red cape, they wouldn't have missed a beat. They were there for words of wisdom and were counting on me to deliver them.

I still remember how my shoes echoed as I walked onto that wooden stage, each footstep taking me closer to admitting my own failings. I stood there and watched the expectant faces in the audience. I saw the hands holding on to notebooks and pens, ready to take down every nugget of advice.

I stood up there and said the last thing any of them was expecting. I admitted my own limitations: "Look, I've got a confession to make," I said. "I'm a failure. I can't close. I'm a bad salesman."

The crowd burst into laughter. Everybody was laughing, cracking up. I had to wait what seemed like an eternity for them to stop and calm down. They thought it was the funniest thing they had heard at the whole conference.

I continued: "I'm serious. Dead serious. I crunched the numbers and I know where I am. All of you look at me because I'm number two in the company and think I'm so successful. Relax, because I'm not as good as you think."

Now they were listening, reluctantly believing me. I could see it on their faces. If I felt I was a bad salesman, how good were any of them? I was there to tell them how to become better and, instead, I was telling them I wasn't good enough. If I was sure I couldn't close, how good at closing was each of the advisors in that room?

I wasn't there to let them down. I was there to challenge them. I was there to challenge myself as well. At the end of my talk, I made a vow. "When I'm here next year, it's going to be a different story. I'm going to make it my mission over the next year to learn how to close," I said.

"Next year, I won't be telling you I'm a bad salesman. I'll be telling you how much better I've become." That was what they needed to hear. That wasn't just my promise. They knew I was expecting the same from each of them. But as a leader, I was first demanding excellence from myself. But to get better, I knew that I'd have to find an approach that fit my low-pressure style.

> I decided that I'd have to give up being a salesman and become an educator instead. It was the only path for me.

Education Is the Best Sales Tool

I was the financial advisor who was cerebral. I had a list of credentials that earned me the spot on the stage. I had my master's degree in financial planning. I'm a Chartered Financial Consultant (ChFC), a Chartered Life Underwriter (CLU), a Chartered Financial Analyst (CFA), and a Certified Financial Planner (CFP).

All of that was great background. Sure, I'm a numbers guy. But my problem was that I had been talking over everybody's head. I couldn't talk anybody's language. Clients love that you have all those credentials. But they still need simple, basic investment advice, not advanced classes in financial theory.

What followed was an education like I had never had. I set out for a year to do it—to take those complex concepts and boil them down into terms most investors could grasp. During that time, I read and studied any book about sales I could get my hands on. I figured out those traditional industry strategies for handling clients didn't work for me or the people I was helping. Financial advisors are taught to hard sell. Once you give a client a presentation and let her go home and think about it, you're going to lose her.

You're taught you have to close them right there. I felt that was too high pressure. I didn't feel comfortable advising clients that way. If they had an objection, I'd overcome it. After two or three objections, it became too forceful. That wasn't my way.

I had to have a process that fit my personality, one that was more laid back but could still convince people the right course of action to take. I spent that year crafting a solution that worked without having to become the heavy-pressure salesman. That fit my worldview much better. It wasn't sales. It was education. Call it the School of Soft Knocks. I'd explain things in layman's terms so that my clients could help me manage their money and their goals. It was the kind of education most advisors would never consider. I was convinced clients would make the smart decision 99 percent of the time—if they'd been given the right information and the right education.

It made me feel more comfortable with what I was doing.

The clients loved it.

That speech in 2001 was one of the most pivotal events in my life—for me and for my clients. Because of it, I went from being just a numbers guy to being someone ordinary investors could put their faith in. I went from being an advisor to being a leader. I was leading from the front, expecting others to follow. A year later I was onstage again, standing in front of many of the same faces.

They were waiting for the great reveal, like when you're watching a mystery movie and sitting on the edge of your seat eager to find out who committed the crime.

This time the speech was entirely different. It was like a victory lap. I was back reporting to them that everything had gotten completely better. It was from June 2001 to June 2002 that I really discovered the educational process that I still use today with clients. That's where I distilled all that I had learned into *my* system.

I took everything my mentor Rick had taught me so many times, only I realized I needed to change it slightly, so that it worked for me and my clients. That's when I came up with something I thought was better.

That event taught me more about how to live and work than you can get in a year of school. It taught me how to tear myself down and build myself back up, better than before.

Leaders Don't Follow

"Being myself" has been part of my lifetime practice. I've repeatedly used the same strategy. I learn the rules first but then I break them.

That's what I did when I got into bodybuilding. I did what everyone told me to do until I figured out what worked better for my body, what worked best for me. That's what I did with my financial model.

Take a look at the financial section of any bookstore or scroll through the pages of Amazon.com. There's a mountain of advice about how to buy stocks for mega-returns. There's very little sane and rational advice, designed to help you get steady returns without putting your whole future at risk.

My way of doing things is different. It combines doing the principled thing and putting my clients first, even if I earn a bit less. It's about making sure my client's money is as conservatively invested as it can be and still earns a good return. My way is educating people. That's how I help lead them, by first teaching them.

Many of my clients have been out of school for decades. They are smart, successful people. But helping them learn and unlearn isn't easy. It's not the time in life where they are expecting to go back to school.

Picture yourself just a few years from that golden retirement—there's golf and travel or just time with your grandkids. You've saved $1 million. It's not a fortune, but with the equity in your house and your Social Security, you figure it will suffice.

Then a market event comes along. Maybe it's another war—perhaps in the Middle East, which never seems to lack them. Or maybe it's just momentum and the people who were buying are now selling. The result is that your $1 million is now $500,000.

That retirement you were eager for is no longer a sure thing. Just to get back to even, you need your investments to jump 100 percent. Sure, that happens. But sometimes it takes decades for it to happen. By that time, you might be eighty, eighty-five, or even ninety years old.

I wish I could say it could never happen, but it already did, in 2000 to 2002 and again in 2008 and 2009. The markets lost approximately 50 percent of their value or more.

What would you do? Would you postpone your retirement? Pull out of the market to save some of what you had?

Those are questions you should never have to answer if you are willing to be a leader with your own money. Do you feel compelled to follow the Wall Street crowd? Or are you willing to take a different path? That's where I come in. My strategy aims to minimize that risk before the disaster ever occurs.

Again, the goal is for you to enjoy your retirement, to have the money you need to live a happy life, free of worry. It's my job in this book to lead you toward that enjoyable future.

A Good Leader Knows When to Change

America gets a lesson in leadership every time there is a presidential campaign. No matter what political party you support, aspiring candidates (and there are a ton of them) constantly jockey for what they think you want to hear. And a few of them tell you what you need to know.

That's the difference between a panderer and a leader. Leaders don't check to see where the polls are or what their staff wants to do. Many people play things safe; they like the routine of their jobs and their lives. A leader has to shake things up either because they aren't working or because that leader can see something new coming down the pike.

As Americans, we're counting on whoever wins to try to lead us and unite us. Like many people in the finance field, I tend to be more conservative on fiscal issues. I understand wanting to help people. I get it that many people idealistically want government to get involved and solve everything. But in the real world, just like in a typical household budget, the money has to be there before good deeds can be done.

The problem is, it all adds up to a few trillion dollars we can't afford.

That's the problem I have with the Affordable Care Act (ACA), also known as Obamacare. I understand the altruistic motive of providing health care for everyone. But you don't do it in 2010, when the country is economically distressed and trying to climb out of the financial crisis.

What Washington bigwigs won't tell you is that every major program we've ever put out cost more than the government projected initially.

To institute the ACA at a time when we were at maximum deficit just wasn't wise. A few years and countless court cases later, Obamacare is still there. And so are the deficits. The United States

Dave and his mom, *"Big Irene."*

Dave, Dad, and Mom; the early days.

Dave during his show on Newsmax TV's *The Income Generation*.

Dave on Fox Business' *Cavuto Coast to Coast* discussing "The Flash Crash", August 24, 2015.

EURO   1.0903
YEN   122.30
POUND   1.4988

BREAKING NEWS

STOCKS RISE ON RATE HIKE

13:11   1.02 ▲ 1.53   Mobileye NV (MBLY) 39.98 ▼ 2.98

CLOSING BELL

CNBC   HD

Dave on CNBC's *Closing Bell*, December 16, 2015; Janet Yellen raised interest rates.

Dave and his favorite guest, Steve Forbes, after an interview on *The Income Generation*, January 2016.

Getting the message out, thanks to the media!

Dave's "*Big Fish*" story.

overspends by hundreds of billions of dollars each year. And our national debt is over $19 trillion.

Neither party has a viable plan to address either of those issues. That isn't leadership.

The same goes for our economy. The federal government plays an enormous role in the economy and often creates excessive optimism.

Just watch the news. During secular bear markets like this one, government officials are quick to emphasize how America is heading out of recession and into a recovery. Investors and voters are happier when the economy appears to be recovering—whether it really is or not.

Those pronouncements always impact investor behavior. Put the president or the head of the Federal Reserve on TV talking about prosperity and recovery, and people plow money into the markets. Then stocks go up, convincing everyone that the markets are fine.

But in a secular bear market like this one, the Federal Reserve interaction could temporarily make the markets go up more than is justified by the economy. In my show *The Income Generation* (Newsmax TV), I refer to that interaction as being on "economic steroids." This caused the stock market to continue its upward cycle after 2013. The market flattened out in 2015 and the beginning of 2016 and eventually will turn downward. Yet again, investors will be left holding the bag. Who has an answer about that?

The president? Congress?

Whoever it is, it will be too late.

No one really wants to hurt the markets, or the economy, and certainly not investors or voters. That would be self-destructive.

The problem is the Fed has gone beyond its original charter and has begun making interest rate policy decisions based on stock market sentiment. The Fed has many critics and rightly so. It's not supposed to prop up the stock market.

Its job is to control the strength of our currency, control inflation, and stimulate the economy during recessions. Now the Fed has incredible power. You don't have to be into conspiracy theories to be concerned about a powerful body that isn't elected.

There is a laundry list of complaints against the Fed—from continuing to make moves that could devalue the currency, to hurting savers, to bailing out big banks.

Then there's a wealth effect. When the Fed institutes policy that makes the market go up, suddenly everyone feels richer. Therefore, people are likely to spend more money and stimulate the economy because they feel wealthier. So, the Fed can indirectly stimulate the economy by propping up the financial markets. This is what happened in 2013 and 2014.

The Wall Street Bull

Unfortunately, most stock market analysts and financial advisors don't get it. They jump on any sign that says recovery or anything close to it. That's because Wall Street would rather talk about cyclical markets than long-term reality because that lets them be optimistic more often, so they can sell more of their products and generate more fees and commissions. Some Wall Street firms will tell you that their number one priority is to help you grow your money. It's not. Their top priority is with the firm's shareholders. Not you. You're an income stream, not a priority.

Let me stress that again. *You are an income stream. Not a priority.*

The CEO's fiduciary responsibility is to "maximize shareholder value," not the value of your portfolio. Ironically, your goals would be better aligned with the firm as an investor in the company than as an investor whose money is managed by the company.

Let me explain. CEOs increase shareholder value by making a profit. If you are a profit center, then it's their job to profit from you, not to make sure you profit. Their first goal is to gain and retain customers. And the second is to keep those customers invested in the markets as much as possible in order to maximize fees and profits for the firm.

Let's face it, people invest when they are optimistic and pull out of the market when they aren't. Out of necessity, the top goal of Wall Street "leaders" is to speak as optimistically as often as they can so that their company makes a profit and their shareholders are happy.

Take a hypothetical case. Go back to early in the year 2000 and suppose the CEO of one of the top Wall Street investment houses had the same information as me and knew we were going into a long-term secular bear market. Imagine the CEO had gathered all of the investment firm's brokers into a giant hall for a major announcement. The room was filled with smiles. The markets were going well. All the brokers were hoping for bonuses or some perks that would make their lives even better.

Imagine the CEO marched onto the stage of that hall, looked around the room, and explained in somber tones that we were entering a twenty-year secular bear market. The crowd would have been silent, their jaws slamming onto the floor, as their boss tells them that investors would see wild ups and downs for maybe two decades, but zero growth.

Money men and women would be standing there trying to envision what to do. Should they find another firm, another line of work entirely? Pull their own money from the markets? There would be a tidal wave of murmurs coming from the crowd as the brokers' fear took shape.

Then picture that CEO going one step further, telling the assembled brokers that they shouldn't put their customers in any more stocks or mutual funds—for twenty years.

The reaction would have been swift. The CEO would have been fired or resigned and moved into some sort of treatment facility for a mental breakdown. The new CEO would have rallied the troops and put them out there selling. The board of directors would have breathed sighs of relief. A crisis had passed.

Had they kept the CEO, the company's profits would have plummeted. Its own market value would have been destroyed. There might have been a sweeping reaction, with investors pulling out, saving themselves billions that would otherwise be lost in the dot-com crash that began later that year.

But again, Wall Street cares about Wall Street, not Main Street. And unless you work in one of those fancy offices or own shares in those firms, they aren't in your corner.

It's not the fault of your advisor, either. It's most of the Wall Street training out there and the research that backs it up. Independent advisors can avoid this trap and learn to think for themselves—learn to be leaders, not followers. It helps when they don't automatically assume that the party line from New York has anything to do with reality.

I've told all this to clients before, and the reaction is usually stunned silence. There's a financial system in this country that we all take for granted is working for each of us.

Only it's not.

That means a lot of very smart people—Wall Street executives, analysts, pundits, and prognosticators—are often misleading you. It's not necessarily malicious in nature; they are just followers, not leaders. If you can't count on them and turn to them as leaders, you need to find better financial leadership somewhere else.

That's why good independent advisors aren't just money people. They are businesspeople. The men and women of the Advisors' Academy, for example, run their businesses from soup to nuts— renting office space, hiring people, doing marketing, making sales calls, and managing money. Entrepreneurs are leaders who learn to question everything.

Those are skills that require more than just managing your money. They require doing their own research to understand a wide range of circumstances. Small businesses are customer focused. They have to be. They know many small businesses fail. They also know you can go to someone else to manage your money, so they provide leadership.

Wall Street isn't the same. If you want to invest in stocks, it's the only game in town. It doesn't matter which of the big brokerage houses you put your money in; they want it in stocks or mutual funds where they make the biggest commissions/fees. That's why we've launched our own registered investment advisory firm— Sound Income Strategies (soundincomestrategies.com)—to fill the gap using our own independent research.

Common Sense Out the Window

Wall Street has abandoned a commonsense calculation about how much you should have in stocks versus bonds. It's one of those back-of-the-envelope numbers that impresses ordinary investors. It's quite simple really:

> Traditionally, 100 minus your age = the percentage of your assets you should have in stocks.

It appears that Wall Street has replaced that simple equation with one that serves their need to sell more risk-based products and charge more fees.

Look at this little quote from CNNMoney's "Ultimate Guide to Retirement":[1]

---

[1] CNNMoney, "Ultimate Guide to Retirement: What's the Best Allocation for My Age?" http://money.cnn.com/retirement/guide/investing_basics.moneymag/index7.htm

The old rule of thumb used to be that you should subtract your age from 100—and that's the percentage of your portfolio that you should keep in stocks. For example, if you're 30, you should keep 70% of your portfolio in stocks. If you're 70, you should keep 30% of your portfolio in stocks. However, with Americans living longer and longer, many financial planners are now recommending that the rule should be closer to 110 or 120 minus your age. That's because if you need to make your money last longer, you'll need the extra growth that stocks can provide.

Many media outlets do this, not just CNN. *Forbes* magazine uses the new 120-minus-your-age rule, and I love *Forbes*. In fact, Steve Forbes has been on my show several times to talk about Corporate Myopia and the state of the markets. Business Insider uses the rule of 110 for men and 120 for women, because women tend to live longer. Many media sources say in one way or another that it's a simple rule.[1]

But let's say you are fifty years old and you think the market will show no growth for twenty years. Why put 50 percent (the old rule) or up to 70 percent (the new rule) in stocks? That's financial insanity.

That's why it's important to be a good leader and be willing to question the norm, or to work with someone who can do that on your behalf—someone who has your best interests at heart, not the interests of a mega financial company.

Business Owners Relate

Many of the clients I work with are just like me—small-business people who have committed their whole lives to a company and an idea. They might be salespeople, dry cleaners, restaurateurs, or home repair professionals. They have a lot in common with each

---

1   http://www.businessinsider.com/equation-invest-in-stocks-2014-12

other because they want to bring some sanity to their financial lives. They've worked sixteen- or twenty-hour days earning their nest egg, and they don't want to risk it.

They relate to me and to the advisors with whom I work because they can see financial core values that match their own. Those come from the top, and I had to learn them from the school of hard knocks. Entrepreneurs are leaders because they aren't the best followers.

The problem with being a start-up entrepreneur is that your company is your baby. Like any good parent, you dote on that child. When it's your baby, you become a perfectionist.

Steve Jobs was a perfectionist; he made Apple successful in his own image. When he passed away, that was immediately how those he kept close remembered him. The tech website CNET talked about him being a "tireless perfectionist who learned from his mistakes." Both Oracle CEO Larry Ellison and Pixar Animation Studios President Ed Catmull said that it was Steve Jobs's greatest strength. Ellison even compared Jobs to Henry Ford for his impact on the industry, saying, "That was Steve, until it was perfect. And then once it was perfect . . . he moved on to the next problem."[1] Alas, I'm no Steve Jobs. Few entrepreneurs ever are. But we share a lot in common, whether we are managing a one-person operation or running a business that changes the world for decades to come.

Leadership and Management

Like most modern businesspeople, I had spent a lot of time trying to be politically correct. We read the books and they tell us that good managers—good leaders—are gentle to their staff and find the right ways to say things to people.

1   Steven Musil, "Execs Remember Steve Jobs as a Tireless Perfectionist," *Tech Industry*, May 30, 2012, 7:45 PM PDT, http://www.cnet.com/news/execs-remember-steve-jobs-as-a-tireless-perfectionist/

Sometimes that has its place. Most of us spend more hours with our coworkers than our loved ones. So managers have to make the workplace as pleasant as possible while still getting the job done.

But successful entrepreneurs understand that can't always be the case. I remember the way Rick used to tell people the hard truth. He'd say it in front of people and everybody would start laughing because he'd say it bluntly. He was direct because he knew what he wanted and knew what he expected. He demanded excellence from people and got it.

I've become clearer saying it my way, just like Rick did. And if that means calling out someone who didn't do a good job, so be it. I'll do whatever it takes to get the point across. Because the job isn't about me or any of the 100-plus people who work with me. It's about the clients and their needs. If I have to step on toes to get those problems addressed, then I do it.

I think if you want to be a good leader, you need to surround yourself with thick-skinned people who can take your personality.

That's decidedly not politically correct. All the books about leadership and being a leader try to show leaders what they should have done differently in a given situation. That's all great. Sometimes it's even helpful. But I've learned that what you create has to be based on your fingerprint, your personality.

> That's why it's important for business owners to hire employees with similar core values. It's also important for investors to hire financial advisors with similar core values.

I discovered my personality is tough. Successful small-business people are all tough. They have to be.

When I got close to fifty, I took stock of my life. I think we all do. I asked myself, "Let's say I've got twenty really productive professional years left. What do I want to do with those twenty years?" That's part of the reason I've been getting more relentless in the management of people.

Relentless doesn't equal mean. It means expecting nonstop excellence, even demanding it.

I've gotten to the point where I want to do it my way. That's the hallmark of the entrepreneur. This is my way. This is the way I've built my business. This is the way I've managed to take care of thousands of clients or customers. And those clients or customers deserve that level of excellence. That's leadership that clients and employees all can understand.

I hire staff and managers who know other ways, and I'll listen to something different if they can make a compelling case. But my way has worked in building this business; their way would have to be either most likely better or potentially a lot better than mine.

Before I got to this point, I would say, "Let's follow a proven path to successful growth of this business. Let's find the proven path and do it that way."

> I later learned that success is more about knowing when to follow the proven path and when to blaze your own path.

As I've said, I've developed my own personal formula for success. It begins by following the proven path in a particular area until I know it well: In other words, I start out by exercising coachability. Then, I decide whether to continue on the proven path or whether to blaze my own trail: That's where the leadership comes in. Many people think that being coachable and being a leader are diametrically opposed opposites, when ideally they go hand in hand.

Leaders won't just lead their organizations. That leadership can be seen when they are among groups of friends, at church, or at their sons' or daughters' schools. They can't turn it off, and that annoys people sometimes.

Entrepreneurs are the same people who demand quality. Thomas Edison, Ray Kroc, Steve Jobs, and Warren Buffett all pushed for excellence from their employees and their businesses. That's why we know their names. They led with excellence as their battle flag.

Investors have just as much right to expect that excellence from those who advise them as from the companies they choose to invest in.

> An advisor is only as strong as his ability to determine when to follow the path and when to deviate from it for the client's benefit.

Graduating from the School of Hard Knocks in My Personal Life as a Follower

Life is about learning the hard way.

We go through kindergarten, grade school, middle school, high school, and often college or graduate school. Financial advisors especially collect degrees and certifications like some people collect coins, stamps, and art.

But the most useful knowledge comes from life experiences, not textbooks.

The only problem is, the lessons we learn the most from are the ones that are most painful. Working in finance is especially challenging. Too many sleazy characters are drawn into finance by the lure of the quick buck.

It took time and pain for me to learn how to spot such people. There can be hard lessons to learn when you watch thousands of dollars go up in smoke because you misread another human being. That's why I value ethics so greatly.

Early in my career I made the mistake of going into business with a builder, a high school friend I foolishly trusted. I was taken for about $100,000, most of which was money I borrowed from people I knew. This guy was twenty-three or twenty-four, driving around in a Ferrari. I was lured by the style, the panache, the idea that he was as successful as he looked.

I was young. Even though it didn't pass my sniff test—or that of others—I fell into that trap because I let greed take over. Thinking he was successful, I felt I could help finance him on his real estate deals with money I borrowed. I was a follower.

Unfortunately, it wasn't long before things took a turn for the worse. Mr. Ferrari, as I called him, had one excuse after another why our company was doing poorly. He told me there was one person in California who owed us money. If we could get paid by him, then we could get things going again. I was becoming very suspicious. I got on a plane and flew to California, determined to sort things out. Remember, it was $100,000 I had at risk and I was only twenty-three years old.

This was long before the Internet. I was going to go to every city to research this fellow's name on library microfiche. I'm stubborn. After several days driving around California, I found him. I walked to his door just as it was getting dark. I was determined to get that money or find out the truth.

I knocked and said who my business partner was. Oddly, he didn't seem surprised. He said, "I'm sorry to hear that," which was my first clue that things weren't what they seemed. I asked him for his help and he invited me in to hear the story.

He sat me down and said he'd be right back. In minutes, he walked back in with the canceled check. "I paid him," he explained. There was disgust in his voice. His interaction with my business partner had clearly not gone well.

That was all I needed to see, to wake up. This experience confirmed what I had suspected for months. That's when I came back to Connecticut and visited my attorney, who put a lien on my partner's house. First, my partner tried to talk me out of it. Then he spent two and a half years in federal prison for trying to burn his house down for the insurance money.

What a fun way to start my career. It taught me to be a leader, not a follower.

Being a Follower Can Cost You Big-Time

It also taught me to listen. One of the great mistakes of life is hearing what we want to hear. This is the same problem with the stock market. Advisors talk about big returns and we hear what we want, not market reality. We don't just let ourselves be taken. We actually help.

Most people have internal suspicions about Wall Street, about advisors, and about how all that works. But we bury them deep and believe the media hype. Just like I fell for the hype with that one-time business partner. I heard the positives and promises. I ignored my gut. I let the greed take over. I followed.

Too many stock investors do the same thing. They downplay the negatives and the risks. That's why good advisors tell people that they could lose all their money investing. That things could go bad somehow.

But human nature is what it is, and we tend not to hear the downside. We hear the pie-in-the-sky beautiful return every time. We never hear the warning.

Boy, did I learn that lesson.

I wasn't the only one. The father of a friend of mine was taken by a so-called investment advisor for a couple million dollars around the same time as my fiasco. He was a wonderful man. He spent his whole life working hard and taking care of his family. Here he was at retirement age and down millions of dollars.

Instead of bemoaning his own losses, he sat me down to talk

to me about my loss. Here's a man who might not be able to retire because of what happened to him, and he's counseling me. He said, "You know, be grateful it's only a hundred thousand dollars. Be grateful you are young enough to recover." Then he gave me this fatherly look that he probably gave his kids every time something went wrong. And he added, "Make it a mission in your life to make every mistake in the book, but once and only once. Learn from this, so you don't turn into me." Now, that's leadership!

What could I say? I took his lesson to heart. I etched it somewhere in my brain. Yes, I make my share of mistakes. I just don't keep repeating the same ones. There's a great expression: "Fool me once, shame on you. Fool me twice, shame on me." I think whoever wrote that had gone through something like my friend's dad.

Following a Follower Can Also Cost You Big-Time

Breaking into any field is always tough. The first five years of my career provided a real shot in the arm of real-world knowledge. Some days, I think it was more like a punch in the mouth.

I think most people start their careers with a lot of hard knocks learning. I sure did. And not all of it involved serious money. Some of it was just knowing that something I was told wasn't right.

I remember working as an insurance agent. I had only been with the company six months, so I wasn't supposed to know much. The company sold a traditional whole life insurance plan in which a death benefit was guaranteed to be paid to beneficiaries provided that a stated premium was paid annually to the insurer. Then the company started up a universal life product as well.

The idea of universal life supposedly involved flexibility, so it sounded great in theory. You could raise your premium or lower it. You could do the same to your death benefit—raise or lower it. You could do almost anything.

It didn't sound right to me. I kept thinking, nothing's for free. I can lower my premium but there has to be an issue with that. In the back of my mind, as an employee of this insurer, I always knew that my bosses would prefer me to sell the products that were most profitable for the company.

Basically what this new product did was transfer the risk back to the insured. If the policyholder was able to change the premium, so could the insurance company. This was 1987, when interest rates were a lot higher. That meant universal life insurance cash values were projected out at 10 percent. When you projected out at 10 percent interest, it looked like you could pay half of the whole life premium and it would last forever.

Remember, I'm a numbers guy. I always do the math. I knew if you took that 10 percent down to 7 percent and expenses didn't get reduced, the product was going to self-destruct. It didn't make sense. Because there is no such thing as a free lunch. I started questioning it, asking the bosses if the plan had been thought through.

It was apparent to me that it was another way for the insurance companies to get out of the insurance business. Insurance companies do it all the time. If you have a claim, they drop you. They don't want to insure when there's risk. They want to insure when there's no risk. This is a way for them to transfer the risk back to the insured.

My objections were not mainstream. Everybody in the insurance industry was going from whole life to universal. I decided early in the business not to jump on the bandwagon. I decided to stay with the traditional whole life insurance. I didn't feel good about the new universal life product. If outside observers were following my career, they might have spotted this as an early sign of leadership. Leaders often don't follow the crowd.

Sure enough, several years later, these policies started to self-destruct as interest rates went down. That hurt a lot of clients, people who thought they had life insurance for life and they didn't.

For younger people who were still healthy enough to get alternate insurance it didn't represent a big problem. However, I spoke with many who bought this type of insurance on the brink of retirement. They had traditional pension plans that provided them with a guaranteed monthly retirement income (the type of portfolio I recommend). They had a choice of different income amounts depending on whether they chose guarantees for their lifetime only or took a reduced option to include their spouses. Many chose to take the maximum income option that paid for their lifetime but not their spouses' lifetime, if their spouses survived them. They often bought these insurance policies to protect their spouses should they die first. By the time many of them realized these policies were self-destructing they were in their seventies or eighties, so they were either uninsurable or left with premiums for coverage that they couldn't afford.

In retrospect, I'm proud that I didn't allow myself to be sucked into this type of product. Just because my company was teaching me to sell universal life plans, that didn't mean I was going to do it. I had been able to provide my clients with the leadership I wanted and they deserved.

I think it was easier for me to be taken when it was just my money. I was willing to take the risks. When it involved other people's money, other people's lives, I wasn't going to let them be hurt. My overprotective nature helped me learn early how to protect my clients. It made me better able to sniff out the BS.

Learning When to Break the Rules Is Essential to Success

Every good leader has to know when to break the rules and when to follow them. I know, you're thinking: If you can break them, what good are rules then, right?

Wrong. Certain rules are the way we structure our lives—work and personal. We obey the speed limit (or we're supposed to) so that everyone is safer. Otherwise, we might have one person doing 120 mph and another person doing 30 mph. We use rules to hedge against disaster.

Now imagine your wife is in labor and you are racing to the hospital. You might not do 120 mph, but you probably will do 80 mph and not worry about getting a ticket.

Knowing when to break the rules is essential to success, but only once you've learned and follow the rules long enough to know the difference. Remember, you have to be coachable before you become a leader.

I remember studying Rick's seminar years ago. I wasn't just studying it. I was memorizing it. Every word, every gesture, every tic. There'd be a point where Rick would make a point and he'd tilt his head on the video. I would make the same point and I would do the head tilt. I was almost superstitious, that if I did one little thing different, I would fail.

I paid attention to every detail so that I would know how to do what he did. I wanted to do it exactly like him dozens of times. Only then, when I had done it exactly like him those dozens of times, did it become part of me. That's when I said to myself: "Now I can break the rules and start tinkering. . . ."

I have done that my whole life. I did it even when I was working out, becoming a gym rat first and then a champion bodybuilder. I discovered that the diet that worked for me and my body wasn't the diet everyone was promoting.

I realized that a no-carb diet was better for me than the diet of high carbs, moderate protein, and no fat that was popular at the time. That's when my weight loss and muscle growth really kicked in. I realized even as a teenager that I would follow conventional wisdom until I knew enough to tinker with it. I knew that only once I mastered the conventional method of doing something and tested and measured the results could I then change it to better fit me.

The same strategy applied when I saw the dot-com crash coming, and again when I looked ahead and saw the 2007–2009 crash coming. I didn't just follow the pack. Packs have a bad tendency to turn from wolves into lemmings very fast. And I'm not one to walk off a cliff.

Breaking Rules Can Save (Financial) Lives

If you've ever seen the TV show *House*, you know what I mean. It's a medical drama and Dr. Gregory House, played amazingly well by Hugh Laurie, is a brilliant oddball. Forty-seven doctors might be convinced that a patient had a bad heart, and he'll be the one who questions that diagnosis. In many ways this show is a great metaphor for life. There is more in life that we don't know than we do know, especially when it comes to medicine. All doctors must go to traditional medical school, but the good ones learn how to question the parts of the medical field that are unknown. That's why in business I always say that it's important first to be coachable and then to lead.

The show was always pulling out obscure illnesses that looked like other problems. Typical medical show, right? Wrong. In real life, a "German man with severe heart failure, fever, blindness, deafness, and enlarged lymph nodes went to a medical center for undiagnosed diseases," according to *Time* magazine.[1] The illness confounded every doctor except one who had watched the show and diagnosed the patient's cobalt poisoning within five minutes— all because of an episode of *House*. It was the result of bad material from a hip replacement. A life saved because of a fictional character who liked breaking rules.

1   Kate Knibbs, "Man's Life Saved Because His Doctor Watched 'House,'" Time.com, February 7, 2014, http://newsfeed.time.com/2014/02/07/mans-life-saved-because-his-doctor-watched-house/

That's why you need rule breakers as part of your financial team. They think creatively when unusual events strike. But if you want to find rule breakers, you ought to know something about the rules that advisors are taught in order to get your business. You will learn a few of these later in this chapter.

My philosophy is much different from most. I broke the sales rules my industry set down, and I have learned that if you take time to educate clients, those clients will always make the right decision. I broke the industry's asset allocation rules by teaching investors that "buy-and-hold" stock market investing doesn't work in the midst of a secular bear market. Wall Street didn't like it, but my clients did. That's leading.

Educate prospective clients and they know what the right decisions are. My process when I meet with clients is to teach them. When I teach them about problems that they have in their portfolios, most of the time they agree that they need to make changes.

Then I educate them about different financial advisor business models. Most of the time, what we find is that the reason these people have problems in their portfolios is because they went to advisors who had business models that didn't fit their needs.

It's not the fault of the advisors. It's Wall Street. The honchos in New York built the system. Most advisors are just reluctant to go against it. They simply need the proper education.

Education is the ultimate rule breaker for Wall Street. Investment CEOs are right to fear it. Because when people learn the truth about the financial industry, when the veil is pulled back for all to see, they often choose a safer, saner path.

The Good News Is There Is Always a Choice

No matter where you look in the world, it's easy to see trouble.

Let's go back to the turn of the century: the bursting of the tech bubble, 9/11, the war with Iraq, Al-Qaeda, then the financial crisis, ISIS and the rise of global terrorism, Greece defaulting, North Korea, Russia and Putin (again).

On the domestic front, Americans seem more divided than any time since the sixties—either the 1960s or 1860s, depending on how you view things.

It all sounds bleak—only it doesn't have to be.

So in some ways, the world always sounds depressing. The more we know about it, the worse it seems. You don't see your evening newscast filled with stories of faith, hope, and charity. Journalists pick murder, mayhem, and war because sizzle sells.

The world has always had a hefty share of both kinds of stories. Before communications became instant, we waited months or even years to hear the news from afar. And then we only heard the highlights.

We focused on our own nation, our own families, our own faith, and our own lives. When you narrow things down, life seems remarkably remarkable.

We have technology no nation has ever had and few people ever dreamed possible—information on everything at our fingertips. Plane travel lets us see the world faster and cheaper than our parents could. Medical advances let us live longer, better lives. The expression that fifty is the new thirty isn't far wrong. (And I certainly hope it's so.)

Even on the investing front, things aren't all bad. Yes, Wall Street is its predictable selfish self. The difference is, it used to be the only game in town for most investors and it's not anymore.

I want you to think about your own life. Imagine having investments you didn't need to check every day. Imagine if the heartache of watching a stock plummet were to simply disappear.

Investing doesn't have to be what you've always been taught. Investing doesn't have to be a painful, crazy roller-coaster ride. The Stratosphere Hotel has a ride on the roof that dangles riders 866 feet above the Las Vegas Strip. They call it "Vegas without a net." That's the way many of my clients view the stock market.

Investing doesn't have to be that way anymore.

I've been telling you throughout this book that there is a simpler, safer way of investing. A way that might help you keep investing, have a stable portfolio, and still grow your nest egg.

I've led you this far. Now let me take you farther in your education.

Learning the *New* Basics of Investment

There are three basic categories of investments: conservative, moderate, and aggressive (see Figure 6). You've spent most of your life learning about aggressive investing; you just didn't realize it.

Aggressive instruments are those primarily invested in for growth or capital appreciation. This is the model most advisors use today. As the chart shows, they include things you are familiar with such as common stock, stock mutual funds, speculative real estate, and commodities.

Again, these instruments are typically invested in for growth or capital appreciation, not income. They're considered "aggressive" in part because it's a simple fact that sometimes when you invest for gains you get losses instead. Think back to our last two major market drops and you'll know what I mean.

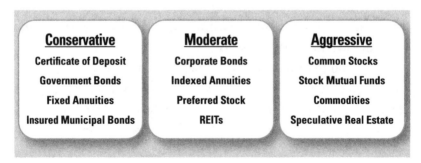

Conservative	Moderate	Aggressive
Certificate of Deposit	Corporate Bonds	Common Stocks
Government Bonds	Indexed Annuities	Stock Mutual Funds
Fixed Annuities	Preferred Stock	Commodities
Insured Municipal Bonds	REITs	Speculative Real Estate

(Figure 6—Basic Categories of Investment Risk)

On the left of the chart are investments that are considered "conservative" because they are insured by a government authority or fund; in theory, they are deemed to have no default risk. They all have a guaranteed interest rate and guaranteed return on principal at maturity. They include bank CDs, government bonds, fixed annuities, and insured municipal bonds.

In the middle are "moderate" instruments that have some default risk or don't guarantee a fixed interest rate but are generally considered to have a much lower risk of loss than "aggressive" investments. These "moderate" options include noninsured municipal bonds, corporate bonds, indexed annuities, preferred stock, and Real Estate Investment Trusts, or REITs.

The instruments on the left and in the middle have two things in common: 1) They're considered, to some degree, to have less risk of loss than the things in the aggressive category, and 2) they are things that people invest in primarily for income.

In other words, they are not things that people typically invest in first and foremost for growth—instead, they are used to generate income in the form of interest and dividends. The interest and dividends that are typically yielded by the vehicles on the left and the middle of the chart represent a way for you to generate reliable income. With most of them, the income stays the same even if the investment itself drops in value—which can give peace of mind for all, but especially for retirees, depending on that income stream. They also provide a way for you to grow your money "organically" through the reinvestment of the interest and dividends that you may not need for income.

This is the approach to portfolio growth I mentioned earlier in Chapter 2. In this scenario you aren't crossing your fingers and toes hoping for capital gains to provide growth; you are building strategically through a method of growth that's more predictable.

In all, that's more than a dozen different categories for investment. Add in the many national and international markets and countless companies and currencies and you can see why it has gotten difficult for ordinary investors to manage their own money unless they have a strong internal leadership sense of what is right for them. Most stock-based advisors invest in things geared to growth—the right-hand part of the chart. Investing in bonds or bond-like instruments is a departure from the kind of investing you've always known.

Look at the investments on the left and the middle of the chart. If most of your previous experience has been investing in the stock market or mutual funds, those probably look as foreign as a Martian landscape. If they do, then it's time to educate yourself or find a leader with the right expertise that you trust.

It's All about the Income

Advisors who specialize in income-generating instruments tend to be few and far between, as most advisors follow Wall Street's stock-market-based model. Those with this specialty, however, typically work more with individual bonds and bond-like instruments than with bond funds.

That's because when investors buy an individual bond, they have two important guarantees: a fixed rate of interest for the life of the bond, and the return of their face-value investment upon maturity. Both guarantees obviously assume that there are no defaults, but with that assumption, investors know exactly what they are going to earn on the individual bond if they hold it to maturity. Moreover, if the bonds being held do drop in value, the interest income stays the same.

That is the kind of result you can't get in the stock market. If it's part of your overall strategy, it can help you reduce the stress of investing.

Bond Mutual Funds

By comparison, interest rates on bond funds aren't guaranteed and can fluctuate. And bond funds have no fixed maturity date. If they end up not maturing, then, obviously, you can't hold them to maturity. There is no guarantee you can get your face-value investment back. In short, the two guarantees that mitigate your investment risk in individual bonds don't exist with bond funds. That's important because there are many factors that can cause bonds and bond mutual funds to fluctuate while you hold them.

With all that in mind, imagine you're a client of an advisor who specializes in individual bonds. Meanwhile, your friend Joe is with an advisor who's put him in bond mutual funds. Let's say something happens in the bond market to cause bond values to drop. A bond mutual fund and a portfolio of individually held bonds might drop similar amounts in value. But that's not the whole story. As you're in individual bonds, yours is only a paper loss. If you choose

U.S. Stock Market vs. U.S. Bond Market–September 2015

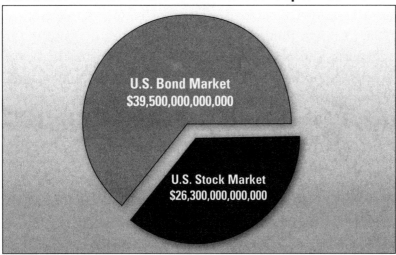

(Figure 7 U.S. Stock Market vs. U.S. Bond Market—September 2015)

Source: http://wolfstreet.com/2015/09/22/bond-investors-get-edgy-bond-market-rout/

to hold those bonds in your portfolio to maturity, then you will get your face value back at that time—again, assuming there have been no defaults. Things don't go so well for Joe, who has the mutual funds. His is an actual loss, not a paper loss. A loss that might have been only temporary in individual bonds can turn out to be an actual monetary loss in bond funds (see Figure 7).

Since that's the case, you might wonder why so many financial advisors use bond mutual funds instead of individual bonds. One reason is that the majority of advisors today specialize in growth-oriented, stock-market-based strategies: those things in the "aggressive" column.

Advisors who specialize in the stock market or the growth side are often not very skilled at fixed-income analysis because it's not their specialty. It's easier for those advisors to recommend a bond mutual fund than a portfolio of individual bonds. They don't have to know the bonds; they just rely on the fund manager to pick the individual bonds.

Bond funds are a simpler way for stock-market-based advisors or even do-it-yourselfers to invest in the bond market. That's how they are advertised, and Wall Street makes bond funds sound good.

But like most things in life, simplicity comes at a cost. In this case, that cost exposes you to significantly more risk. That's why experienced fixed-income advisors often skip bond mutual funds in favor of a portfolio of individual bonds.[1]

The Right Education

Like everyone else in America, you've been raised on stocks, stocks, and more stocks. It's almost as if we all watched the movie *Wall*

---

1   Wolf Richter, "The US Bond Market Is Far Larger Than the Stock Market: If Even Part of It Blows, It'll Dig a Magnificent Crater," Wolf Street (blog), http://wolfstreet.com/2015/09/22/bond-investors-get-edgy-bond-market-rout/

Street and internalized only the profits part of the picture and not all the related problems. You've been misled. The big investment houses have been leading our nation away from safer investments and toward aggressive ones where they can make the big bucks.

It wasn't always that way. More than thirty years ago, conservative financial investment alternatives were extremely popular with retirees and those nearing retirement. Everything changed during the last bull market of the 1980s and 1990s. When investors became addicted to the stock market, more rational investments were labeled as "dull," "boring," or "old-fashioned."

That means very few investors even understand their alternatives. Most have, at best, a basic understanding of these investment strategies without any real-world knowledge.

Again, building your wealth by receiving predictable interest and dividends from your investments is what I call a bird-in-the-hand approach. It's a smarter alternative in today's environment than crossing your fingers and toes and hoping for capital gains—which can quickly become losses.

Roller-Coaster Rides Are Fun, but Not for Your Money

Investing is often based on fear and greed. I want to lead you in a different direction. I want you to set those aside and invest in hope.

I want you to pick what are the most important things in your life—your faith, your family, your physical and mental well-being. I want *those* to be the dominant forces in your life. Investing shouldn't dominate your personal time. It shouldn't overwhelm you and worry you.

Investing is a tool. But to too many people, it has become a pastime—like fantasy football or the way kids used to memorize baseball statistics. If you truly get enjoyment from that, knock yourself out. I do this for a living and that's not what excites me. I enjoy helping people achieve their goals. And while I like a good math exercise, that's not enough in life.

Investing should provide you with what you need to retire, to care for your family, to do the things that make your heart sing.

I've spent much of this book detailing the problems of the stock market and giving advice on how to find someone to help overcome them. This is part of the heart of my message about how you can overcome Wall Street and accomplish things on your own. You don't need to follow their leadership. They are taking you in the wrong direction, like a Pied Piper.

Wall Street is terrifyingly out of sync with the investors I know. Most people are tired of the big investment companies making huge money off of people's terror.

DAVE'S TIP NUMBER 5:
Trust Your Investing Instincts— or Trust Someone to Act on Your Behalf

You've been misled.

Oh, it didn't seem like it at the time. The world played an awful game of follow the leader. Some people made outrageous fortunes. But there's a good chance that you and millions like you were the ones who got led off a cliff.

Leadership is a double-edged sword. History is full of great leaders—just as it's full of villains. The investment field has both as well; we just seldom hear their names. We might hear about their companies, but their companies are some of the top firms on Wall Street.

The September 2015 issue of the *Atlantic* examined "how Wall Street bankers stayed out of jail" after the 2008 financial crisis:[1]

---

1 William D. Cohan, "How Wall Street's Bankers Stayed Out of Jail," *Atlantic*, September 2015, http://www.theatlantic.com/magazine/archive/2015/09/how-wall-streets-bankers-stayed-out-of-jail/399368/

Since 2009, 49 financial institutions have paid various government entities and private plaintiffs nearly $190 billion in fines and settlements, according to an analysis by the investment bank Keefe, Bruyette & Woods. That may seem like a big number, but the money has come from shareholders, not individual bankers.

By October 2015, CNBC reported that "fines and settlements amount to $204 billion paid out through 175 settlements since 2009."[1] Three months later, "The Wall Street firm of Goldman Sachs . . . agreed to a civil settlement of up to $5 billion with federal prosecutors and regulators to resolve claims stemming from the marketing and selling of faulty mortgage securities to investors," according to the *New York Times*.[2]

Like I said, misled. By Wall Street.

Leadership is power. It's also responsibility.

Ask Yourself

1. Are you the kind of person who doesn't hesitate to zig when others zag? Or do you feel comfortable implementing something only after you know that others are also doing it? (Doing this too often could mean you have a problem with authority and make you less coachable, but doing it occasionally shows leadership qualities.)

2. Do you have good instincts for recognizing when something doesn't pass the sniff test? And if so, do you trust your instincts enough to take action? (If you answered

---

1 Jeff Cox, "Misbehaving Banks Have Now Paid $204B in Fines," CNBC.com, October 30, 2015, http://www.cnbc.com/2015/10/30/misbehaving-banks-have-now-paid-204b-in-fines.html

2 "Goldman to Pay Up to $5 Billion to Settle Claims of Faulty Mortgages," *New York Times*, January 14, 2016, http://www.nytimes.com/2016/01/15/business/dealbook/goldman-to-pay-5-billion-to-settle-claims-of-faulty-mortgages.html?_r=0

yes to both, you certainly have leadership qualities; the question is, do you have enough to be the sole manager of your life savings and retirement?)

3. Have you ever had a hunch or gut feeling that some investment was about to go up or down, but you failed to act because it went against popular consensus or recommendation?

It's that same spirit of leading that compelled me to found the Advisors' Academy and, later, Sound Income Strategies (SIS). Anyone can stand on the sidelines and say this is what's wrong with Wall Street. That's not my personality. I went into business to be a leader and that's what SIS is—a leader among registered investment advisory firms.

Ask your advisor these questions:

1. If your advisor works for a larger firm, ask: "How much financial research do you do personally and how much research is supplied to you by your firm?" (Some who work at larger firms are leaders and tend to do their own research rather than relying on others or their firm because they realize the bias of some of the existing research; they also exhibit diligence.)

2. If your advisor operates independently, ask: "How do you compile your research?" (By asking an open-ended question you can determine whether the advisor "gets" the research from another source or prefers to do research on his or her own.)

3. "If I heard about a great stock opportunity and I wanted you to put me in it right away, how would you respond?"

4. "Tell me about an important time in your life or career when you strayed from the pack and led others down the road less traveled."

Don't hire someone who tells you investment rules are like holy writ. You want a leader who will actually advise you based on real-world circumstances and common sense. You don't want someone who gives investment advice as if reading it from a textbook. Textbooks get outdated. Advisors can't.

That's why I decided to add tips and questions at the end of each chapter, to help you spot a bad advisor.

PRINCIPLE

6

FINANCIAL HONESTY

The Wolves of Wall Street

In *The Wolf of Wall Street,* Leonardo DiCaprio plays a twisted, soulless investment broker whose sleazy behavior earns him mountains of cash. He throws it away in search of an expensive lifestyle, on hookers, and on an endless supply of illegal drugs.

No, Wall Street isn't like that. It's a Hollywood stereotype designed to sell movie tickets.

But I can't say Wall Street is completely honest, either.

I just can't.

Many feel the Wall Street game is rigged against the little guy. Even though I have tons of friends—ethical men and women—who work in finance, I understand that sentiment.

According to the Chicago Booth/Kellogg School Financial Trust Index, Americans don't trust the financial industry anymore. The survey of more than a thousand "financial decision makers" showed that "despite Americans' anxiety over income inequality, they do show increased trust in credit unions, with some 60 percent of respondents saying they find credit unions trustworthy; only 30 percent say they trust big, national banks, which tend to be for-profit and invest in financial products that are unfamiliar to many Americans."[1]

They have good reason to feel that way. A terrifying 2013 survey of the industry, titled "Wall Street in Crisis: A Perfect Storm Looming," The results of the Labaton Sucharow survey showed that a large percentage of respondents agreed that their competitors engaged in unsavory behavior as written about in the Jordan Thomas article "Wall Street in Crisis: A Perfect Storm Looming," July 16, 2013.

Wall Street has more than just an appearance of impropriety. In November 2014, "regulators fined six major banks a total of $4.3 billion for failing to stop traders from trying to manipulate the foreign exchange market, following a yearlong global investigation," according to Reuters.[2]

The six banks were

- HSBC Holdings PLC
- Royal Bank of Scotland Group PLC
- JPMorgan Chase & Co.
- Citigroup Inc.
- UBS Group AG
- Bank of America Corp.

Recognize any of those names? You should. It's difficult to bank anywhere in America without them. Reuters noted the "fines bring

---

1 "Chicago Booth/Kellogg School Financial Trust Index Reveals Public Concern over Income Inequality, Broken Education System," press release, September 2, 2014, http://www.chicago booth.edu/about/newsroom/press-releases/2014/2014-09-02

2 Kirstin Ridley, Joshua Franklin, and Aruna Viswanatha, "Regulators Fine Global Banks $4.3 Billion in Currency Investigation," Reuters, November 12, 2014, http://www.reuters.com/article/ us-banks-forex-settlement-cftc-idUSKCN0IW0E520141112

total penalties for benchmark manipulation to more than $10 billion over two years."

If you bank at any of those institutions, you paid for it. The fees they charged you and the profit they make off of you as a customer—that all went to help pay the fines. On Wall Street, that's just the cost of doing business.

It's Not Just the "Bad" Guys, It's Everyone

Wall Street players now have primarily one goal—making money for themselves. Forget the customer. Forget the businesses they are investing in. Their goal is to keep you invested because they lose their profits if you move out of the market.

Wall Street cheerleaders try to brainwash you to stay invested. Then they come up with some sort of ridiculous example where they depict someone who doesn't obey their strategies as a loser. Many of the major companies try this strategy. They try to make you feel stupid if you don't stay invested. It's like they learned from the captain of the *Titanic*. If water was flooding up over their knees, they'd still say there was nothing to worry about.

These are creations of their marketing departments. In one such advertisement, they depicted an unlucky guy who had held a portfolio for ten years but got antsy and wouldn't stay put. He tried to time the market, pulled out, and then jumped back in. Naturally, he foolishly missed the ten best days in that ten-year cycle. So he would have made much more money if he had stuck to a buy-and-hold approach. Instead, he sold and made much less. The moral of the story is always the same: buy and hold.

They say: *Don't think. Just give Wall Street your money.*

What they don't discuss is the other side of the argument. They don't want to encourage anyone to think. I did. I wondered years ago, just for the sake of argument, what if he had missed the ten worst days instead of the ten best? I went back and did the math in one sample. The difference was about three times as great.

The math stunned even me.

If you listened to the brokers, you risked too much by getting out even if only for a few days. But if you did it their way, you wouldn't have missed out on gains by leaving the market. If you missed the worst ten days, you would have saved three times as much as you could have made on the upside. Avoiding downside risk was three times as important toward reaching your goal.

The point is simple. Wall Street brokers weren't being intellectually honest. These creations are designed to keep you perpetually in the markets. That worked for a long time. For example, to best manage a mutual fund, the fund manager needs to have a gauge for expected inflows and outflows. Nothing messes up a fund manager's mojo worse than unexpected inflows and outflows.

With the arrival of the Internet, news started to travel at a more rapid clip and day traders emerged. Investors actually started to day-trade their mutual funds. Wall Street was ready. When mutual fund families couldn't brainwash people anymore, they just changed the rules. The companies started adding restrictions on how often you could move your money from one fund to another. If they can't brainwash you to buy and hold, they'll force you to buy and hold.

I Call It "Wall Street's Cancer"

The cancer can spread like a virus through an entire organization. It spreads down from the CEO to the research manager to the sales manager and then to the broker. Everyone gets infected. Everyone gets greedy. Clients are no longer customers; they are a means to an end—and the end being the goal of maximizing company profits.

Sadly, it doesn't stop at the Wall Street firms. It spreads from them horizontally through the media—news outlet to news outlet, all saying the same thing, all interviewing the same people. Few members of the media are willing to discuss the problem because the media make a majority of their money through advertising these same firms. The price we pay for subscriptions barely defrays the cost to deliver the information.

Look at the places where the media get some of their research. Sometimes they are interviewing investment pros, whose own companies did the research and issued buy or sell orders to their clients. Now they push that research out, promoting their position, giving strength to the buy or sell order and making the firm look smart.

Reporters also end up interviewing their own advertisers. If a journalist interviews an advertiser, the result may not be trustworthy. Sure, that reporter gets the research done more quickly and gets to quote someone who might be with a big Wall Street name, even if it's also on the list of paying advertisers.

The advertisers will love it. So they'll probably advertise again next month. Then the whole cycle starts over again, while it continues to spread.

Next it goes from Wall Street and the media to the very schools that teach financial advisors. Often, the same Wall Street firms started the schools and donate money to help keep them afloat.

I don't want to make it sound like it's a conspiracy, because it's not. It is simply how capitalistic markets function. I couldn't imagine living in a socialist country, and I hope that everyone reading this book is happy to be living in a capitalist society. Whereas there are lots of great benefits to living in a capitalistic society, nothing in life is inherently good or inherently bad. If capitalism didn't have any negatives, socialism wouldn't even exist. This is one of the unfortunate negatives of capitalism. Investors need to realize this when reading or watching the media discuss financial issues; take everything with a grain of salt and, again, question everything. Be brutally honest with yourself.

Everywhere up and down the line, the story is the same. From business schools to investment houses to the news outlets that count on them for information. There is only one right way to play the game. You have to play it the way Wall Street wants you to. You buy stocks, you buy mutual funds, and you stick to their playbook.

No one questions it because most everyone is part of the game somehow. Analysts won't question it for fear of losing their job. Media producers won't question it because the paying advertisers need to be comfortable with the overall media message; reporters and writers won't question it because their job is to produce content at lightning speed for the producer that is in line with that media outlet's message. This might just be the negative part of our most treasured freedom—freedom of speech. Again, when anyone can say anything in a global society, an investor needs to question everything and everyone when it comes to his or her money. If you are not willing to do that, you need to find the right advisor to do it on your behalf, and even that may be easier said than done. Let me give you a depressing example.

More Hard Knocks

When I was getting one of my financial certifications, I was being taught a lot of modern portfolio theory, or what I call "financial alchemy." The courses were all about how you mix together different investment classes and subclasses and come up with some sort of magical equation to mitigate risk.

It sounds convoluted, but we took it very seriously. It's kind of like when you take deadly hydrochloric acid and the deadly alkaline substance sodium hydroxide and mix them together. The result you get is saltwater, which is relatively harmless unless you are shipwrecked.

We were taught that assets work that way in the investment world. When you mix together small-cap and large-cap, domestic and foreign, and growth and value stocks, you can also mitigate that volatility risk. It's a foundational theory every advisor has to learn.

When I was getting my credential, Long-Term Capital Management (LTCM) was the biggest hedge fund. It had two economists on board who had won Nobel prizes on this topic of "financial alchemy," and they were earning big checks using their knowledge for this hedge fund's strategy. That's why the LTCM became huge. Nobel prizes are a pretty nice marketing edge.

These fund founders had another advantage. By choosing a hedge fund they had fewer regulations than mutual funds. They set up a complex trading system based on the differences between short- and long-term interest rates on bonds. If their mathematical models detected a narrowing or widening between those different types of interest rates, they would change their portfolio allocation. The firm soon had billions of dollars in assets and was leveraged heavily.

It also didn't work. When financial markets didn't perform quite the way the trading system counted on, it started spiraling downward. In less than a year, LTCM lost $4.4 billion out of the $4.7 billion it had. As a study of how ineffective these strategies are, I opened up the *Wall Street Journal* in August 1998 and there was an article about how Long-Term Capital Management failed. I was reading firsthand about the flaws in these methods.

These were the same strategies based on financial alchemy being touted in my courses. So I called the teachers and asked them how I should study for the exam. I said, "I'm kind of between a rock and a hard place. Do I pay attention to what the book told us or do I go by what's happening in the news?" I was told to go ahead and study what's in the textbook. They didn't have time to change the exam.

That's what I did. Obviously, I passed.

But if you went for your designation today, it's still the same financial alchemy being taught. (A book, *When Genius Failed*, by Roger Lowenstein, goes into the fall of LTCM in depressing detail.) I understand why. Financial alchemy can actually work in a secular bull market. These strategies can help avoid harm during small pullbacks.

The same can't be said when big, unexpected events occur—what are known as "black swan events"—such as 9/11, Chernobyl, the Internet bubble, or the financial crisis of 2008. When events get that bad, just when investors need those tools to protect them the most, that's when they fail.

That happened in 2000–2002 and in 2008. It didn't matter if you had large-cap, small-cap, domestic or foreign, or growth or value stocks. They all dropped. Everything was dropping at the same time.

It's human nature to see patterns in everything and look for reasons to justify them. Statisticians call this data mining, and this financial alchemy is just one example. Investors and advisors alike had a false sense of comfort in many of these theories—again, underlining the importance of being brutally honest with yourself.

It's like the 100-year flood. I live on the waterfront, and everyone always talks about what happens if you get the 100-year flood. Most people don't live near water their whole lives. And even if they did, they might miss out on a 100-year event. Meanwhile in 2008, financial advisors were dealing with the 100-year flood in the markets and they didn't even know where to go to find a bucket.

Investing through the Rearview Mirror

Another human tendency is to feel comfortable investing only after we've seen an elongated run-up in price. Psychologists call this hindsight bias. Everything was going down in 2008. Then the stock market reversed, starting March 9, 2009. Almost everything was going up through 2014 and then 2015 landed right in between, with almost no change. During 2013 and 2014, however, the upside proved just too tempting for a lot of investors who had been sitting on the sidelines, trying to be patient. They gave up and finally jumped in, but only after the market had fully recovered and broken through its previous peak levels from 2000 and 2007.

It's because when things are going up, we all hear what we want to hear. We become euphoric. When there's a piece of bad news and a piece of good news in a euphoric period, the market ignores the bad news. The good news sets the tone for the market. I know that makes no sense. Just chalk it up to human nature.

There are so many threats to the markets out there that no one wanted to discuss from 2013 to 2014: the geopolitical crises including Greece and China, the collapse of Detroit, and Puerto Rican debt. And all that forgets a pretty substantial point: that the Federal Deposit Insurance Corporation (FDIC) was still holding a lot of housing inventory that hadn't flooded the markets yet—a real risk to housing values. What was different this time was that by 2015, a lot of people actually felt like the markets' high level just didn't make sense. They knew it in their gut. It even crossed political boundaries. Before, it was only the Tea Partiers who thought something was wrong. They were right to complain about our burgeoning national debt, which is over $19 trillion as of this writing. By 2015, almost everyone was starting to realize the markets were irrational and no longer made sense.

Again, being honest with yourself, if you can resist these psychological tendencies, then good for you! If not, perhaps you should consider finding an advisor who can help protect you from yourself. But don't automatically assume that all advisors can protect you in this way. Let's face it, financial advisors are human too and have to fight these same tendencies. But I urge you to have an honest conversation about it either way.

Don't Settle for Less Than the Whole Truth

I don't doubt for a minute that there are Wall Street analysts smarter than I am. There are bound to be. They hire some of the best and brightest out of the best schools from around the world. They can afford to. The New York State Comptroller reported that the Wall Street bonus pool was $28.5 billion in 2014. The average bonus was $172,860 per person. I'm sure that every Wall Street firm had analysts smarter than me who could have done the very same data analysis that I did—research that takes into account not just forty or sixty or eighty or so years of the markets. I mean research that includes 200 years of market history. If they actually did this research at the investment banks in the 1990s, they chose not to talk about things they considered inconvenient.

Most brokers were given stock market data back to 1926; therefore, they were left to decipher only two big secular bear market cycles in the twentieth century. The first was 1929–1954 and the second was 1966–1982 (see Figures 8 and 9). Brokers naturally discounted the first of those two bears as having to do with the Great Depression. New rules and regulations would allegedly prevent a crash that big from happening again, so the theory went.

Based on that thinking, there exists only one "normal" secular bear market for analysts to extrapolate from, and that's not enough of a trend from which to identify anything useful. So the convenient solution for analysts and brokers alike was to throw up their hands and declare that the markets were random and unpredictable. In this case, they would have to encourage investors to buy and hold so that, God forbid, they didn't miss the ten best days.

Brokers have consistently ignored somewhere between 60 and 75 percent of market history. Is it any wonder they often seem flummoxed by events?

That's what I mean by honesty. It's not just about lying or telling the truth. It's telling the whole truth that's important. And Wall Street isn't doing that.

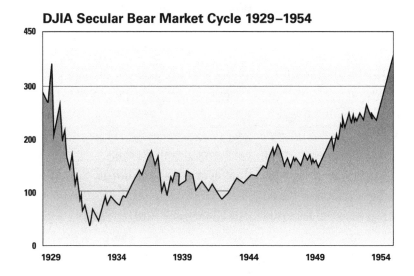

(Figure 8—DIJA Secular Bear Market Cycle 1929–1954)

Source: http://www.multpl.com/s-p-500-historical-prices/table/by-month

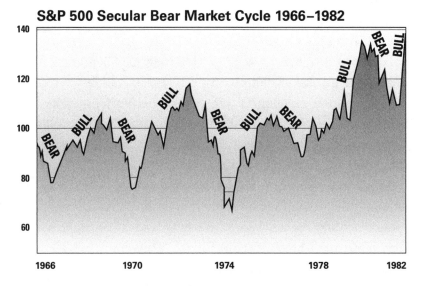

(Figure 9—S&P 500 Secular Bear Market Cycle 1966–1982)

Source: http://www.multpl.com/s-p-500-historical-prices/table/by-month

Doing Well by Doing Good

I saved one of my most important lessons for the end because it's all part of how we plan our legacy—taking care of those we love. It's appropriate, since we are talking about the golden years, to talk about the Golden Rule: Do unto others as you would have them do unto you.

In the business world, that translates into ethics.

Ethics fall into a special category. They're not just an essential quality for a good advisor. They're also something you need to find within yourself to move forward into the future.

It's important to take stock of your life as you plan your retirement, just like I did after my mentor Rick's tragic death. How do you want to be remembered? What do you want to accomplish while you have both the resources and the wherewithal to do it?

I've been telling advisors for years that this job is about helping others, not just about making money. Those who understand that do well. Those who don't get found out by their clients sooner or later. They are building their houses on sand. The Bible is very clear on that. It doesn't work.

Founding members preach this to the new members at the Advisors' Academy. The academy is an old-school operation, comprising advisors around the country who value honesty and integrity. Our financial model teaches how to do the right thing for the clients. It's not about selling the products that generate the highest revenue. It's about doing right for the right reasons.

That outlook has drawn a lot of advisors who have strong traditional values of faith and family to work with us. Many of them come from smaller markets where faith and doing right haven't been blotted out by our media culture. They are drawn to us, as some would say, like flies to honey.

When you do the right thing, you learn the business better. You market better. You run your business better. That results in you doing more of the right thing. It's a self-perpetuating cycle. When you do the right thing, your clients make more money. Though you might make less per client, you attain more clients. Which means you actually end up earning more.

I think men and women who care about doing right tend to gravitate to us in large part for those reasons.

We had a study group with a bunch of advisors at our Florida headquarters one time, and while I was listening to a conversation I realized they were discussing their concerns about the school system. We went around the table and seven of the ten people we were mentoring homeschooled their children. While homeschooling has become popular in all walks of life, they made the choice because they wanted to make sure they could teach their own children the definition of right and wrong.

On another occasion one of those seven was talking to me about doing right and how it had changed his view of being a financial advisor. He said something that really stuck with me. "I thought this business was a way to make money so I would have free time and resources for my calling," he said. "But this *is* my calling! I'm helping people in so many ways, and it never sank in before."

I smiled. I was pleased that he finally got it. I asked him to think back to our study groups over the years and said that's the message I've been trying to get across to him for five years.

I could hear the smile in his voice. He said, "Yes, yes, I've got it. Finally got it."

That made my heart glad.

Ethics vs. Rules

I don't think we learn ethics as adults. We get it as kids by following the Golden Rule. But kids need more; they need specific rules to follow. But as adults trained to follow rules, we find that conflicts can exist between rules and ethics. I've learned that the hard way over the years.

In 2002, something occurred that pushed me into becoming an independent advisor. I jumped in with both feet. In the course of doing the right thing, I almost had the government land on me with two much larger feet.

It was just before Christmas and snow was already all over Connecticut. My assistant was taking time off (because my name isn't Scrooge) but work still had to get done. One client who had gotten a life insurance policy through me decided he *might* not want to keep it. I didn't see that as a problem because I don't do pressure sales. It was early enough in the life of the policy that he would receive no cash surrender value. However, I recalled that he had already paid more than the required minimum premium, so his insurance coverage could continue for a while with no additional payments. Surrendering it now would be no advantage for him because he would lose insurance coverage he had already paid for. I explained that it meant he didn't have to rush the decision and we could get together after the holidays to discuss it. If he still wanted to make a change at that time, he certainly could.

As always with financial advice, it's up to the client, not the advisor. I told him I'd make a call to verify everything. If I'm correct, I asked him, "Do you want to wait?" He said, "Yes." He said he wasn't going to be home but asked me to leave a message on the answering machine. I called the home office and they told me there was enough already paid to switch him to annual payment mode, just as I expected. This meant that in essence, he could have free coverage for a couple more months. I called him and left him a message that I had great news: "You're good to go. I'll call you after January to make a final decision." Another happy customer.

Then reality hit. I got a call from the home office a couple of days later and they said they had made a mistake. They told me the client had to come up with $400. I explained to them that wasn't how it worked. They made a mistake and they had to make good on it.

I'm sure you've heard this one before. They said, "We can't do it. It's against company policy." That put my ethics up against their stupid policy.

I didn't like following phony rules, so I told them: "Well, I'll come up with the $400. I gave the client my word." That didn't work either. They said they wouldn't take my check. Again, against company policy. I said, "Fine," and hung up. I figured that if I just sent them a check, they'd never know or care who sent it. A $400 payment magically went into the mail and I forgot all about it. That let me relax and have a great Christmas with my family, knowing I did the ethical thing.

January came around and everyone was back at work. Someone in the company processed the money order and called me up. They asked if I sent the check. I wasn't going to lie. I said I had. They had said it was against their policy, but they understated the case. It turned out it was against a regulatory authority regulation. I felt my stomach drop to the floor. I had unknowingly violated some regulation about which I wasn't aware.

I had been working with the firm since 1987, and they allowed me to do business elsewhere provided they received enough proprietary business from me. I liked my independence, and I did a lot of business with other firms, depending on what was best for my clients. I was probably sending one-third of my business through my firm and two-thirds elsewhere. My firm's primary products were mutual funds and I wanted to put people in safer investments because of the markets. (It was 1999 to 2002—a rocky time.)

Even then, the one-third of business I was sending them was more than most of their advisors sent them. I got to the point where I was one of the top fifty or sixty representatives at the company nationally, even though I was sending some business elsewhere. They wanted me to send them more but tolerated me since I was a top advisor. Tolerated me up until this point, that is.

Now the top men in the organization had an excuse to push me out and make me look bad over something silly. They chose to terminate me because I broke a regulatory rule that they disguised as company policy while I was fixing a mistake that they had made.

Naturally, they also reported me to the regulatory authorities.

This might even have been the end of my story if I had genuinely done something unethical. Thankfully, I had done the ethical thing, even if it unknowingly violated a rule. When the supervising government entity contacted me, we talked about what happened. I was completely up front about what I had done. The man from the government sounded almost apologetic and explained there was a backlog of serious violations where people had *actually* stolen money. My case didn't seem to be a primary focus for him.

That sword of Damocles hung over my head for months until the government man called again and said he had to impose some sort of penalty. We agreed on a ten-day suspension and a small fine. He asked if I had a vacation planned. I did and he told me that I would be suspended during that time. Case closed.

That's how I got pushed out in 2002 to become totally independent. It turned out to be a blessing in disguise, even with all the upset stomachs that little incident caused me. That experience taught me that conflict can exist between honesty (fulfilling what you promised) and rules.

Ethical Behavior Happens Whether Someone Is Watching or Not

Once I was on my own, I decided I could do some work from home. So I decided to make sure that home was in the nicest place I could find. With my love of boating, Florida was as far south as I could go and stay in the United States. It was a place I had always wanted to live. During the financial crisis in 2008, real estate prices were plummeting. With the prices right, I could finally manage that dream.

So I went house hunting.

This was around the time when Bear Stearns failed. I had the money to buy a nice house and a lot of people suddenly didn't. That's called leverage. I found a highly recommended Realtor. I was honest with her. "Look, I'm going to work you very hard, but I'm going to buy a house from you." I meant it.

I started looking at fifteen to twenty houses every weekend. I wanted a nice house, but I wanted a nicer bargain. I had a solution: I'd give low-ball offers two at a time. They were all rejected. I made ten or eleven offers. All rejected. That's business.

Finally, I found the deal I was looking for, in the center of Ft. Lauderdale. I liked the house more because it was a bargain than because it had anything special. It was nice enough.

Weeks passed, and the acceptance period, where if you back out you lose your earnest money, was nearing an end. But I was still keeping my eyes open for houses. It had become a habit. I was in Florida and still visiting open houses—only without my agent. She figured I had the house I wanted, and she was getting things ready for the close.

Then I stumbled on this beautiful For Sale by Owner house right on the water. It wasn't a nice house. It was an amazing house. It had everything I wanted. Above-average frontage right on the water, unobstructed views of the intracoastal, new but not a mansion, so it would still feel like a home. The house hugged the water and had huge windows, a large open kitchen, and lots of room for friends and guests.

I fell in love with it.

I told the owner that I wanted to buy it but had already put an offer on another house. I gave him my best offer and told him I couldn't pay any more. He accepted.

For most people, that's the end of the story. Man finds house of his dreams. Moves in. Lives happily ever after. The Realtor gets written out of that scenario.

Only I had promised. I don't take promises lightly. I went back and calculated how much money the Realtor would have made personally as the selling broker. Then I wrote her a check for that amount. It was over $30,000.

When I gave it to her, she was surprised and confused. "Nobody's ever done this!" she said, catching her breath. I was thrilled that she was happy, but sad that no one ever had simply done the right thing. In her mind, I took honesty to a whole different level. In my mind, I figured I had given my word that I was going to buy a house from her. I didn't, but I did buy a house without her. That meant I owed her for her work.

What good is having an advisor who scores number one in everything else if that person isn't ethical? You know the answer. The unstated part of the Golden Rule is that if someone can't be trusted, then don't let that person manage your gold.

Yet most Americans ignore that rule. They ship billions of dollars to Wall Street despite scandal after scandal. The good folks at *Forbes* made a list of "The 10 Biggest Frauds in Recent U.S. History." I think they limited it to "recent" history because otherwise the list would be too long.

It's a parade of bad actors: Enron; Bernie Madoff, who ran a $65 billion Ponzi scheme (Ponzi was another famous financial crook); Lehman Brothers; WorldCom; and Fannie Mae. And those are just the high- (or low-) lights.

Still we cheer the parade because that's what we're taught.

The *why* is easy. Our society has lost touch with what matters. It's not just chasing the almighty dollar. That you could almost understand. It's a lack of empathy. A lack of ethics that encourages people to pursue their gain, even when it harms you or me.

Ethics remain an essential foundation as you make the decisions you need to make in order to secure your financial future.

Handling Financial Loss

Socrates said, "Know thyself." This is particularly valuable advice for investors—so I say, "Investors, know thine own risk tolerance." Not everyone practices what they preach—but most know inherently that they shouldn't risk more than they can afford to lose. So if another 50 percent loss, for example, would reduce your retirement income or cause you to postpone retirement, then you shouldn't take the risk, period. But what if quantitatively you could afford a 50 percent loss and still accomplish all your goals? That's where Socrates's advice comes in—will you stress over every expenditure? Will you lose sleep over it? Will you allow it to affect your mental or physical health, or will it change your closest relationships? If your answer is yes to any one of these questions, then I recommend being brutally honest with yourself before you subject your hard-earned money to that type of decline.

As we accumulate wealth, many set net-worth goals. When a particular number is achieved we pat ourselves on the back, feeling good, maybe even a little smug. Let's just say, for example, that the goal set was $1,000,000 net worth. The question is, how would you feel at that level if you started with $2,000,000 and incurred a 50 percent loss in the markets? Some of you might naively think you would feel the same at the one million mark, regardless of the direction from which you hit that number. Unfortunately, that's not how most investors react.

Worth Avenue is the Rodeo Drive of Palm Beach, Florida, close to where I live. Bernie Madoff had lots of "clients" there. Shortly after the news broke of his Ponzi scheme, I happened to be walking down Worth Avenue on a Saturday afternoon. Tumbleweeds could have been rolling down the streets; I was startled at the emptiness. I'm sure that most of the reasonably affluent people didn't give everything to Bernie; in most cases it was less than half of their fortune. So what had been $20 million net worth might now be $10 million to $15 million. Most will agree that someone with a $10 million to

$15 million net worth can still afford to shop on Worth Avenue. In fact, I'm sure that most were happy to shop on Worth Avenue when their net worth was rising up and through that dollar level, but not on the downswing.

Be honest with yourself. Be brutally honest with yourself. How would you react if that happened to you? Investing isn't for the faint of heart. If you are over forty, you know too well. You've survived two of the most traumatic times in stock market history.

First we had the dot-com crash in 2000. Our nation went from irrational exuberance to terrifying reality in the space of a few years. Millions of people had jumped into the markets, risking money they couldn't afford to lose on stocks they were told wouldn't ever fall. (see Figure 10)

Fall they did, on a grand scale, taking the tech-heavy NASDAQ down with them. Market events like that undermine your confidence in the system, even if you got out in time like my clients.

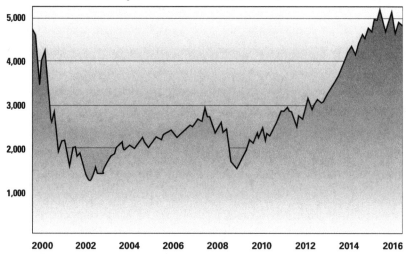

(Figure 10—NASDAQ Composite Index 2000 to 2016)

Source: http://finance.yahoo.com/q/hp?s=%5EIXIC&a=00&b=1&c=2000&d=05&e=9&f=2016
&g=d

It should have been a wake-up call. It should have made investors wise up and maybe even rise up. Instead we had more financial insanity just a few years later.

When the dust cleared after the dot-com implosion, markets climbed and climbed and climbed from 2003 to 2007. Then in 2008 they fell even more spectacularly than before their gains. Nest eggs were gutted, retirements were canceled, and the global economy reeled.

In 2006 and 2007 some people had forgotten the painful lessons they had learned just a few years earlier and bought into crazy Wall Street notions about riding out the bruising ups and downs of the markets. Everyone took another beating if they relied heavily on the markets.

The results scarred veteran investors and advisors alike. I've been calling it a form of financial PTSD, or posttraumatic stress disorder. Then I saw some research that used that exact term.

According to two Kansas State University PhDs, even most financial planners were harmed by what happened. "In the months following the 2008 crisis, 93 percent of the planners surveyed reported medium to high levels of posttraumatic stress symptoms, with 39 percent of planners reporting severe symptoms of posttraumatic stress," they wrote in a 2012 analysis.[1]

For ordinary investors it might even have been worse. Many pulled from the markets because they never learned how to cope with the loss. Young people learned just to stay away. Less than 7 percent of Americans thirty-five years old or under now own stocks—even in retirement accounts.

Other Americans didn't learn how to move past the awful events that had happened to them. Their losses paralyzed them almost literally. Their financial lives were frozen—either in the stock market

---

1   Bradley T. Klontz and Sonya L. Britt, "Financial Trauma: Why the Abandonment of Buy-and-Hold in Favor of Tactical Asset Management May Be a Symptom of Posttraumatic Stress," *Journal of Financial Therapy* 3, no. 2 (2012), https://www.psychologytoday.com/sites/default/files/attachments/34772/financialtrauma-whytheabandonmentofbuy-and-holdinfavoroftacticalassetmanagementmaybeasymptomofposttr.pdf

or out of it. The fear makes them more susceptible to mistakes in the future.

Loss is a traumatic event. Whether doing it yourself or working with an advisor, you need to be honest with yourself on how you handle loss on the upfront. Unfortunately, many of us learned just how risk averse we were only after losing money. That's something we all need to think about. Loss comes to us all because we are all mortal. It's how we cope that counts, how we find the path we need to follow. If we don't manage it, we leave ourselves and our families in jeopardy.

I didn't learn that in the stock market, though I wish I had. I learned that from my mentor Rick. It was the last lesson he ever taught me. It's a lesson I'd gladly give back.

Rick was more than my mentor and my coach. He was my friend.

Don't Let Fear or Loss Paralyze You

He was a classic man's man—brilliant and proud of his blue-collar roots. His six-foot frame weighed more than 200 pounds. Rick was good-looking and kept his hair in a buzz cut, I think as a way of staying connected to who he'd always been.

He never denied his roots. But he was savvy enough to use them to his advantage, to make them part of his persona. As I mentioned before, some advisors were uncomfortable with him because he had a different style. Other guys were motivated by it; they'd look at his haircut and say, "If he can make $2 million a year helping all those people, I can do it, too. If he can do it, I can do it."

They didn't realize the haircut didn't make the man. Anyone in the armed services can tell you that. It's just part of their uniform, as it was part of Rick's. If you stopped there, you missed the amazing man beneath it.

It's been fourteen years since Rick died. He was the man who taught me some of the most important lessons in my career. I guess it's only fitting that I try to make sense out of his death in a way that can help other people, like he helped me.

Loss comes into all of our lives. We all suffer setbacks, encounter crises, and lose loved ones. That's what life is all about. I know in my heart that we can't ever appreciate the good things in life without having the bad. But that doesn't make it any easier.

Rick was a hell of a friend and mentor. He built a business and made sure his family was taken care of. That's the kind of thing he would have told his clients they need to do as well. Plan for the future and take care of your loved ones. Because when trouble strikes, it will be too late to do anything about it.

But remember, trouble does strike. Homes catch fire. People get in accidents or get sick. We lose jobs and our businesses shut down. The litany of problems is enough to make any heart weigh heavy. And I know that's not what Rick would want for any of us.

He counseled countless clients about their money and how to deal with losses and fix past mistakes. Rick knew that eventually every crisis passes. Every pain dulls a bit. How we handle it all is what defines us—in our own lives, including how we handle investment loss.

Rick used to tell me that what doesn't kill you makes you stronger. I don't know whether to laugh or cry when I remember him saying those words. But he's right. I learned so much from knowing him. I even learned about loss from my close friend.

I tried to do what he would have done and turned that negative into a positive. I took the skills I had mastered under his tutelage and founded Advisors' Academy. I wanted my legacy to be helping, coaching, and mentoring other advisors. I think he'd be pleased.

(Almost) All of Us Were in This Together

Writing about loss is one of the hardest things I've ever done. I've been making it personal because there's nothing more personal than the losses we endure in life.

Each time the market has plummeted in recent years, millions of people have been harmed. According to a report called "Cost of the Crisis," the combined cost to Americans of the financial and economic crisis of 2008 was $12.8 trillion.[1] That works out to roughly two-thirds of our entire national debt.

Those are numbers most of us can't comprehend. If you counted once each second, counting to a trillion would take 31,709.79 years. To count to 12.8 trillion would take 405,885 years.

I was tempted to make a joke about that. The number is so staggering. Then I remembered what each of those numbers meant. Each one represents one hard-earned dollar for someone in the United States.

Just one lets you order off the dollar menu at McDonald's. Twenty gets you a pretty decent lunch. Fifty lets you have someone join you for that lunch, with room for a fair tip. In a nation where the median household income is $53,657,[2] those outgoing dollars start adding up fast.

That means the "conservative" estimate for what we lost in 2008 was roughly equal to the total yearly earnings of 80 percent of U.S. households. Homes were lost, and others were dragged so deeply underwater that their owners might never climb out. Even now, as of the end of 2015, RealtyTrac says 11.5 percent of all properties are "seriously underwater" by at least 25 percent.

That number is over 25 percent in states like Maryland, New Jer-

---

1　"The Cost of the Crisis" (Washington, DC: Better Markets, July 2015), https://www.better markets.com/sites/default/files/Better%20Markets%20-%20Cost%20of%20the%20Crisis.pdf

2　"US Household Income," *Department of Numbers*, http://www.deptofnumbers.com/income/us/

sey, Florida, Nevada, and Illinois. Many of those homeowners will never be able to sort out that mess without incurring further losses or walking away. This has forced millions of Americans to be honest about their own risk tolerance.

I'm not going to sit here and say, "I told you so." Instead, I'm going to remind you that you need to find a way to get past it. You need to accept what happened and move on so you can secure your future—so you can take care of your loved ones.

I can see you shaking your head, telling me that I'm crazy. No sane person can just move on from two of the worst markets in one's life.

You're right. But we all find a way to get past the pain of loss. We all have to. It's part of being human.

I know.

I lost the person closest to me—my mom. She was diagnosed with cancer on October 27 and died December 6, 2013.

My Greatest Loss Ever

My mom was on her third type of cancer. She had survived breast cancer and lung cancer. Cancer was tough, but my mom was tough, too.

The doctors caught her third cancer at a very late stage. She had symptoms going back a year and a half, but doctors totally misdiagnosed it. By the time they finally realized she had uterine cancer, it was too late. The doctors said that surgery was no longer an option. They couldn't stop it. My mom, the woman nothing could stop, finally ran into the one thing she couldn't beat.

She had a high pain tolerance. It was that inner toughness she had. But once she went into the hospital, she never came home again. Forty days of misery.

I had lost two of the people I was closest to, had them die with me right there. It was awful knowing that Rick passed away in the prime of his life. This was even tougher.

It's one thing to lose someone you care about in a sudden accident, as happened with Rick. I heard the impact and I'll never forget that sound. But I didn't have to watch, and I did my best to try to save him. I knew I had done everything I could. At least I felt I tried.

It was different with Mom. I actually watched her pass. That was horrible.

Beyond Loss

Our stories don't end with loss. Both Rick and my mom had great lives and impacted a ton of people. I can't just dwell on the loss every day and stop living.

They'd both have wanted to kick my butt if I did that.

I still remember going to Rick's funeral. There were probably 200 financial advisors there. Being a numbers guy, I couldn't help but think that if each of these advisors had 200 clients, Rick affected 40,000 lives favorably in his short forty-five years. While he died before his time, it's a comfort to remember he left an impressive legacy behind. That was a big takeaway from my loss. I decided I would not let it bother me emotionally but instead take the energy and focus it on something that was Rick's dream too. I channeled the energy to do something positive. I decided to not let it destroy me. I did the same when I lost my mom. Tried to live the life she would have wanted for me.

As a mentor to advisors, I've seen some let their lives deteriorate and others let their business slide because of outside events like divorce or a death in the family. That happens because they are unwilling to move on. Investors often have the identical problem.

We dwell on the past—not focusing on the good, but on the loss.

So I'm going to channel both Rick and my mom and tell you to get over it.

If that's tough love, so be it. It's the honest talk we all need to move forward. The candor we need to accept the past. That doesn't mean we don't learn from each loss.

Of course you can't compare the loss of loved ones with financial losses, but there is a similarity in that you have to learn from each loss and move on. As a society, we've been unwilling to do that with the stock market. The markets kick us in the teeth and we keep going back for more.

Death can't be eliminated but financial losses can be mitigated. The best thing you can learn from financial losses is to do your best to prevent them from happening in your life in the *first place* or from happening ever again.

DAVE'S TIP NUMBER 6
Admit What You Don't Know and Don't Be Afraid to Hire Someone Who Does

Be honest. Have you been answering the questions in the tips sections?

I said, be honest. This isn't college or even high school. There's no one looking over your shoulder and no one grading the results. The questions are only designed for you. Nobody else. So, if you don't answer them, the only person you are cheating is you.

You've read this far because you know what I'm telling you makes sense. Financially, you fought your way through two downturns and the worst economic collapse since the Great Depression. It had an effect on you. It had an effect on everyone.

If you were invested in the markets, you suffered an incredible loss—a loss of money you worked your whole life for, a loss of confidence in both yourself and the system, and a loss of faith that America is still that beacon of hope where hard work is rewarded. It's such a profound sense of loss that the only thing I can relate it to is the loss of loved ones.

Believe me, I know too well they aren't the same. But how else do you measure the work of years or even decades of your life?

Now you want to put that all behind you. Now you are considering your future, but you don't know where to turn and how to get wherever you might want to go.

It takes guts to admit what you went through. It takes honesty to admit you don't know what to do now.

Face it: Some of us "can't handle the truth"—to borrow a line from Jack Nicholson's character in *A Few Good Men*. Investing is all about the truth, and facing it is sometimes hard. It means facing up to a failed investment rather than continuing to ride it downward, and understanding that market realities might be different from what you saw on the evening news.

Honesty is even more than that. It's admitting to yourself what you can or can't do. If you've read this far and think that investing for your future is something you are best qualified to do, then you have a hard but potentially rewarding road ahead for you.

You can look forward to reading about stocks and bonds and government regulations every day the markets are open. It would probably be good if you read books, took some courses, and even got yourself some of the formal training that advisors get—because many of the other investors out there have that knowledge base and you don't want to be at a disadvantage.

It's a habit you'll want to commit to daily. Want to take your spouse on vacation? Better be sure to block out some time to handle your investments and read the news. I have friends who play fantasy sports—baseball and football, mostly. They study the players like I study investments, but they do it for fun and their entire futures aren't riding on whether Tom Brady has a good game. Ask yourself:

1. Have you ever lost a large percentage of value in a particular investment because you were waiting for it to come back up in price to what you paid? (This could be a sign that you were unwilling to be brutally honest with yourself and admit it was a bad choice in the first place.)
2. Have you ever had an investment that was increasing in value and you promised yourself that if it got to a particular price you would sell? And if so, when it got to that price did you really sell or did greed kick in? (Self-discipline is an important quality in an investor, so be honest with yourself.)
3. In 2008 or 2009, did you ever vow to yourself that if the market came back and your investments were covered you would get out? If so, did you get out, or are you still in?
4. Have you ever undertaken a project but determined at some point that you weren't really qualified to do the best possible job with it? If so, did you soldier on or did you seek out the best qualified person for help?

Be honest with yourself: Can you admit that?

Because admitting you can't do something isn't surrender. If you are a successful businessman or -woman, you've probably hired dozens or maybe hundreds of people in your career. You hire them because you know the business and know what it needs. They know their specialty. Don't be reluctant to interview financial advisors and ask them these tough questions:

1. "Can you tell me of a time—in business or otherwise—when what you felt was the right thing might have cost you money, but you did it regardless?"

2. "Tell me of a time when you had to be brutally honest with a client about a mistake you might have made or something that was, for whatever reason, difficult to communicate."

3. "Tell me of a time when a client might have had an unrealistic expectation of investment returns or a retirement plan in general. How did you handle it?" (Clearly, you want an advisor who will be brutally honest with you and won't blow smoke.)

4. "Have you ever had a client file a complaint or lawsuit against you? What happened and how did it turn out?"

You should ask and expect your financial advisor to be totally honest with you in all these ways. It is the right thing and the smart thing to do, if you want to secure your financial future. And be honest: Everyone wants to know their money is safe and secure. Yet forward-thinking businesspeople saw how college students and others became engrossed in social media. Marketers saw it as a great opportunity. When they didn't know it, they hired their expertise. Some of what they got was a mixed bag. Who are the experts in a brand-new field? But still, employers were smart enough to know who the experts weren't.

Financial advice has been around forever, but it's still a changing, evolving field. If you don't know enough to manage your own money, then be honest about it and hire someone who does.

7

FINANCIAL FEARLESSNESS

IF YOU WERE to meet me in my private life or come along with me for a day that I'm fishing or flying a plane you might think, "This guy is fearless." And it's true. I happen to like individual sports. But it's important to note that in *every* case I was taught and mentored by someone who could show me the way.

My fearlessness today has a lot to do with my identifying exactly what I wanted to learn first and then planning exactly how I was going to accomplish that goal. I invite you to do the same with this book and with many of the free educational offers you find in the epilogue to this book. (Stick with me for a few more minutes before we get to that. . . . I have an important point that affects both of us.)

I get a lot of enjoyment out of living a life that I truly *want* to live and think others should do the same. If I can make one personal plea in this last chapter it would be this: I would recommend stepping out of your comfort zone in your hobbies and in your leisure time to do what you have always wanted to do.

Think about that for a second. Think about what you've always wanted to do. Imagine swimming with dolphins, taking a cruise around the world, or maybe really spending time with your grandchildren and watching them grow up instead of grabbing a few hours each holiday. Overcome your fears and do those things that mean something to you—even if that means setting aside work for the first time in decades.

With increased leisure time and the wisdom that comes with age, you can afford to be a little fearless. After all, one of the benefits of getting older is that we understand the difference between recklessness and fearlessness and, hopefully, much of the "business of life" is behind us. It's time to solidly plan for that final one-third of life where we get to reap what we've sown.

But we can't relax if we convince ourselves that everything is perfectly fine as is—and that covers a lot of territory. For you to take time and relax during retirement or as you head toward retirement, you have to be honest and admit that everything isn't fine in your financial life. If you've got money in mutual funds or managed accounts that include stocks or exchange traded funds (ETFs) then by definition you have little control over how much that money will be worth in the future. Someone else is managing that money, along with millions or probably billions of other dollars. Your part is just a drop in their bucket.

The difference between fearlessness and recklessness can be found by assessing the amount of control you truly have over your retirement income. It doesn't help to convince yourself or listen to an advisor or broker who still thinks the market "always recovers" and you should stay in it for the remaining 2 percent growth you may or may not capture.

A Lesson Learned at the Grocery Store

Taking control of your financial life is essential and it can start even early in your career. One day, in 1999, I got a lesson in just how out of control the market had become. I went to the grocery store to buy a couple things and a stock boy tapped me on the shoulder to ask financial advice. I realized I was wearing a baseball cap embroidered with the name and logo of a well-known mutual fund family and that probably meant to the young man that I knew something about stocks. Back then, everybody still wanted to be Michael Douglas from *Wall Street*.

I felt bad. Probably no one in his life had given this young man a proper financial education. And he probably didn't get any help at school, either. So he asked me, "Mister, I've saved some money and I'm curious if you think I should buy stock in eBay or Amazon. com." I thought for a second, wondering how to help him. I answered with a question of my own: "Do you have a car?" He nodded with a sense of pride. I asked, "Do you have a car payment?" His smile turned into a frown pretty quickly and he nodded yes. I told him: "I have a better idea. Pay off that car."

Even stock boys wanted to get in on the action back then because they thought it was easy money. Unfortunately, easy money often turns into easy money . . . for someone else.

That was the 1990s. There was a lot of recklessness happening then in the tech boom. Everyone was like that stock boy. They all thought you couldn't lose in the markets.

Period.

In the late 1990s everyone thought stocks and mutual funds were a sure bet, whereas in reality everyone was being reckless but didn't know it.

More recently, since the recovery from the last financial crisis, many investors have returned to a 1990s mentality.

I talk about this when I'm teaching my national workshops. Most investors don't understand that there's a lot more to investing than just picking a good stock or even a good mutual fund. But people read financial publications and all they see are headlines like "Top Stocks to Buy in 2016" or "The Best Mutual Funds for Your Money Right Now."

Don't Blame Yourself

Even people who are reasonably well read on financial issues usually don't know how to differentiate a true financial advisor from a financial salesperson disguised as a financial advisor. Many so-called financial advisors may offer three, five, or even ten preset portfolios. The client may feel like it's a custom portfolio but it's not much different from buying a mutual fund. And worse, these portfolios are typically growth-oriented, not income-oriented. But if this sounds familiar to you, I think I understand why. In fact, in my experience, there are three reasons that this type of mindset is prevalent, even today:

Ask Yourself:

1. Would it be correct to say that you've gotten serious about your investments for retirement during the last thirty-five years? If so, then that means that you've not yet participated for one full market biorhythm. Don't blame yourself, because it makes it impossible for you to realize that this is part of a consistently repeatable cycle.

2. You were introduced to the investment world during the 1980s and 1990s, the best bull market in U.S. history. Isn't it true in life that it is our earliest experiences that shape

our paradigms? For most of you, that means that your earliest experiences were double-digit returns in stocks and mutual funds. Every time you took a little bit more risk, it meant more return. The challenge, however, since the year 2000, has been to change your paradigm, despite those earlier experiences.

3. Chances are, your parents had the privilege of working at the same company for most of their careers and retired with a meaningful pension income. In the 1980s and 1990s, however, you saw those pensions disappearing, and you knew that you had to grow your money. Of course, investing for "growth" makes sense when you want to grow your money. Just like investing for "income" makes sense when you need (or will need) income from your investments within the next ten years. The only problem is that old habits die hard.

Most Americans can probably relate. They turn their eyes to investing, and preserving what they have, when they begin to think of retirement. Those are the clients I work with the most. Unfortunately, before they get to me, many of them are in the dark about reality and often suffer as a result.

That's my purpose talking to you this way. It's the reason I wrote this book and the reason I do my TV show, *The Income Generation*, on Newsmax. I want people to focus on where the markets are today and, more important, not to fall for recklessness disguised as optimism in the markets once again.

My 2007 Concerns Put in Writing

Nothing brings this point home to me quite as strongly as looking at my October 2007 newsletter to clients—even almost a decade later. I was urging folks to rip off the rose-colored glasses and come up with a solid plan to protect their retirement, either with their advisor or as a do-it-yourselfer. Based on what you have learned in this book, doesn't it feel like 2007 all over again? As of mid-2016, the markets have been hovering at nearly record market levels when we know that historically no secular bear market has ended with only two major drops inside of it. Here's what I said in October 2007:

> With the Dow Jones Industrial Average (DJIA) and the S&P 500 both reaching historic highs in July, it would be easy to assume that even greener pastures lie ahead for investors. While that could be the case, it's also possible that other significant trends could come into play in the coming months.
>
> I'm talking about the Secular Bear Market Trends I have discussed with most of my clients over the past several years. I've noted that, during these trends, it is not uncommon for the market to approach or even ever-so-slightly surpass its previous high (see Figure 11).

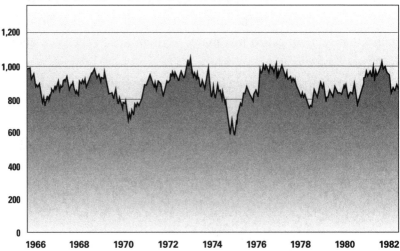

(Figure 11—DJIA Secular Bear Market 1966 to 1982)

Source: https://www.google.com/finance/historical?cid=983582&startdate=Jan%20
1%2C%201966&enddate=Dec%2031%2C%201982&num=30&ei=BvBZV5CMFoOWeezK-
loAP&*start=240*

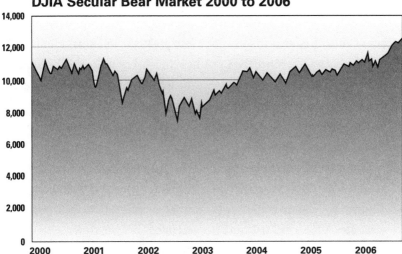

(Figure 12—DJIA Secular Bear Market 2000 to 2006)

Source: https://finance.yahoo.com/q/hp?s=%5EDJI&a=00&b=1&c=2000&d=11&e=31&f=200
6&g=d&z=66&y=1716

Figure 11 shows the 1966–1982[1] bear market and compares it to the first seven years (1/2000–12/2006)[2] of this current trend. You can see that during the 1966–1982 periods, the DJIA approached and even slightly surpassed the 1966 high on several occasions, only to retreat more than 20% each time (see Figure 12).

As of 2016, the S&P 500 and the DJIA went more than 20 percent above the record peaks from the year 2000, although the NASDAQ is just approaching its record peak from the year 2000. You might be tempted to think that we are already in the new secular bear market since the two large-cap indices have gone so high. Here's what I said back in 2007:

---

1   1966–1982 DJIA, https://www.google.com/finance/historical?cid=983582&start,date=
Jan%201%2C%201966&enddate=Dec%2031%2C%201982&num=30&ei=BvBZV5CM
FoOWeezKloAP&start=240

2   2000–2006 DJIA, https://finance.yahoo.com/q/hp?s=%5EDJI&a=00&b=1&c=2000&d=11&e
=31&f=2006&g=d&z=66&y=1716

Now wait a minute, I know what you're thinking. Sure, the graph does indeed go slightly over the previous high, but it ends in December of 2006. Between then and the July peak, the DJIA has climbed 2,000-plus points. Since the DJIA has climbed significantly beyond its previous high, is it possible that the worst is over and the market is emerging into the next secular bull? Of course it is possible, but before you jump to any conclusions, I encourage you to consider the following two points.

First, many fund managers agree the DJIA may not be the best market indicator. Most agree that the S&P 500 is a much better indicator. The S&P 500 represents 500 stocks instead of only 30 (like the Dow). It is capitalization weighted, not price-weighted (like the Dow). . . .

Now you're thinking, didn't the S&P 500 also just hit a new high? True. But it has since fallen back. And even with that peak, it still means that the S&P 500 has just now returned to where it was in early 2000! So an investment in an S&P 500 Index fund (and many mutual funds) has generated zero growth in the past seven years. Actually when you factor in inflation, you've lost ground!

So the second drop finally began at the end of 2007, once both the DJIA and the S&P indices had hit their previous record high levels from 2000. Meanwhile, the NASDAQ was lagging far behind. Now that the NASDAQ has nearly caught up to its record high from the year 2000, while the other two are in record territory, we might very well be poised for that third drop. You might be thinking, though, that price-to-earnings ratios are in the high teens right now, which is only a little bit higher than average. Here's what I said in 2007:

Second, depending upon the method of calculation used by analysts, P/E ratios across the S&P 500 were over 20 as of 4/30/2007—far higher than the average of 14–15. The market did not recover from the 1966–1982 bear market (as well as most previous secular bears) until the P/Es dropped well below the average of 14–15.

I then tried to appeal emotionally to clients who still had that "1990s mindset" with their investments. Here's what I said then:

That's why investing is simple, but not easy. "Buy low and sell high" is simple, except that our emotions often get in the way. Think back to the winter/spring of 2003 when the Dow dropped down to the 7,500 range. Were you eager to buy then? When the DJIA had just dropped 4,000 points and market pessimism was at its highest? Conversely, the market has made great gains recently with the Dow nearing the 14,000 mark. Are you eager to sell now when the market looks so good? You see my point.

Am I saying that you should sell all of your stocks and stock funds tomorrow? Of course not. I'm simply urging you to stick to a sensible allocation and not allow yourself to be lured into a false sense of security. Should the market return to its 2003 low, it would represent another drop of more than 40 percent. Conversely, if it were to take four years to recover again, that could represent several more zero-growth years.

We all know what happened next. Here's how *U.S. News & World Report* described it just one year later in October 2008:[1]

During eight blustery trading days beginning in late September, horrified investors watched the Dow Jones industrial average tumble nearly 2,400 points, including a sickening 18 percent drop in a single week. Pundits began comparing the dizzying fall to two other market plunges, Black Monday in 1987 and the 1929 crash heralding the Great Depression.

That was only the beginning.

---

1   Kirk Shinkle, "The Crash of 2008," *U.S. News & World Report*, October 17, 2008, http://money.usnews.com/money/personal-finance/investing/articles/2008/10/17/the-crash-of-2008

It's a memory we won't soon forget. Often when I'm on CNBC or Fox Business or my own show interviewing or being interviewed by a stock market cheerleader it begins to feel like it's 2007 all over again! They seem to find limitless reasons to sell optimism and keep you invested in the stock market, even when common sense dictates otherwise. My goal is to help you avoid another meltdown and live your later years fearlessly.

Don't Worry, Be Happy! . . . Income is the Key!

If you've worked hard and built up a decent nest egg, this is supposed to be the time to live the good life. Sadly, the world around you doesn't always cooperate. After two market collapses in just fifteen years, I don't know anyone with a lot of money in the market who rests easy—and that includes financial professionals.

It's only natural to be worried about whether you have the money to live out retirement comfortably and travel where you want. It's only rational that parents want to make sure they can help their children attend college or have a nice wedding, maybe even put a down payment on that first house. I manage money for a large number of people from all walks of life and I can assure you that if you plan from this moment forward, you should be able to make all of those things happen in your lifetime. Accomplishing your security goals is just the beginning of tapping into fearlessness—but it begins with taking control and making a commitment to yourself.

It's your money, and no one will ever care as much as you do about your own money. If you are working with a financial advisor, make sure this person respects that fact and works in partnership with you but also can show you some leadership in the process.

You shouldn't have to spend your retirement pacing the floor, worried about every market dip. This is the time you should be relaxing, having a mai tai, and watching the waves roll in on some beautiful beach.

That means you need more than just retirement money. You need a plan that generates enough **income** to achieve your goals, and possibly someone to help you carry it out. Do that right and you can retire without the fear that has dogged your investment life since the time you bought your first stock or plowed your hard-earned money into a mutual fund.

Fear is a funny thing. Being fearless with justification is one thing, but being fearless in a reckless machismo way is insane. You can jump out of an airplane with a parachute, with all the needed training, and feel fearless. Assuming the parachute was packed properly, you have a lot of reasons to believe that nothing bad will happen to you. But feeling fearless while jumping out of an airplane without a parachute is insanity.

Fearlessness comes from knowing that your parachute is packed right and is going to open. If I told you there was a 50 percent chance the parachute would open, would you feel fearless? I doubt it. By the same token, on any given day, there is a 50 percent chance the market will go up or down. That's a statistic that does not help foster fearlessness.

By now, you have read about **investing for income instead of growth**. This is similar to knowing your parachute will open with 100 percent confidence and having fearlessness with regard to your retirement.

Let's face it, what goes up often goes down. Capital gains can turn into capital losses, and growth can turn into shrinkage. Relying on possible gains certainly doesn't make you fearless.

> Those clients I see planning and enjoying their retirement fearlessly have one thing in common: an investment portfolio geared toward generating consistent income in the form of interest and dividends.

My Lifetime Promise to You

Advising people about investments isn't really about the money for me, because I follow my own financial advice. For me, it's about fulfilling Rick's and Mom's legacy, and about helping the greatest number of fellow investors as I can. After reading this book, many of you might want to become clients, but while I have some capacity for growth, I couldn't handle that even if I wanted to.

Remember, I love my life, but life is not all about the work or business. That's why I accepted the offer to host a new television show called *The Income Generation* on Newsmax. Like this book, it's my way of getting my message out and helping all of you while maintaining the same balance in life I want for each one of you. I figure it's better to remind you of the basics while reading a book rather than learning the hard way with your life savings. That should mean that our journey together will continue after today. But only if you want it to. I'll make it painless: Just go to returnonprinciple.com and help yourself. Leave your name and even a note on how you liked this book; I promise I will actually read each and every comment.

I'll do that because I like to stay in touch with what people are thinking. One of the things I find with clients is that they've often had very little conversation with anyone about their retirement. In fact, many seem to view "retirement" almost as something you shouldn't talk about—like it's a disease and you might catch it if you even mention the word.

You should talk about it. You've worked for decades, scrimping, saving, and investing. Those 401(k)s, 403(b)s, pensions, and IRAs all become important. And few people understand how to truly navigate those waters. And if you are going to talk about it, it might help to have someone to talk to who isn't involved.

Meanwhile, relax and start dreaming of beaches (or snowy slopes). Wherever your fantasies take you. Envision that retirement. Envision learning to live without the fear.

You've earned it.

Finding New Goals

In the movie *The Graduate*, Dustin Hoffman's character is given one word of advice to build his life on: "Plastics."

Only that's not a life goal. It was intended as career advice. It might even have worked as investment advice, depending on the companies he chose. But it's not life advice. Plastics aren't life. They aren't a goal. They were intended to be a means to an end.

You aren't at an end. You are at a new beginning.

This book has been about preparing you for that beginning. I've been trying to give you the tools to help you know the opportunities you face.

Now that you have a better understanding of the importance of having investments that generate consistent **income** in the form of interest and dividends during retirement, you're almost ready. But ready to do what?

How about ready to make dreams come alive?

This is one of the parts of life that many people don't understand. We spend our whole lives working in jobs or industries that we let define us. That's a lot easier if you work at what you enjoy, as I do. But it's still work.

Imagine you had your whole life ahead of you. Imagine you had enough money to do some of the things you've always wanted. Now remove the aggravation, the stress, and the terror of standard Wall Street investing.

Think what life could be like if you were less focused on your investments, unbothered by the strain of tracking six mutual funds and twenty to thirty stocks. You'd have all that time to focus on the good things in life, unchained by the stress that hounded you all those years building that nest egg.

Many people choose travel—to see sights they've only read about or seen in movies. I hear clients talk about exotic destinations like the ancient ruins of Machu Picchu or skiing in the Alps when the slopes are as smooth as silk.

Maybe you feel you've earned some solitude and you want a cabin in the woods—filled with good books, good food, and great company.

Some clients do what many of the members of the Advisors' Academy do and devote time to charity. They take the money they've made in life and want to spend time helping others.

Those are all wonderful ideas and there are billions more where those came from.

Personally, I like a challenge. I've always enjoyed competing against myself. It made me very goal-oriented. Fox example, I was in a restaurant one day in a Spanish-speaking country and grew immediately frustrated that I couldn't understand.

I decided to learn Spanish. I know, usually languages are a young person's game, but I'm stubborn. So I started learning about two years ago. One of the first words I looked up was "goal." If someone wants to talk to me, I can't talk about myself as a person without saying the word "goal." That word is my whole life.

That's my goal. Only, it's personal.

I've worked my way through other goals that are standard among many businesspeople I know. I've thought about what I want out of life, just as I want you to. I've decided I want to focus more on life experiences. I love the competition of man versus nature. I guess that's the Hemingway in me, like *The Old Man and the Sea*. And I pursue it every chance I get.

That's a goal worth striving to accomplish.

That's what I mean when I ask you to think about your retirement goals. I'm not asking you to say you want to sit around the house and watch TV. You can do that now. I want to challenge you to be happy with yourself and your life. I want you to live as you never have before.

The idea is that you take the money you've spent a lifetime earning and put it to good use accomplishing a goal you believe is worth striving for. Don't waste the money. More important, don't waste your time, your talent, and your opportunity.

That's what my mother taught me. Not to waste my God-given talents. That's how I want to live—today and every single day I have on this earth.

That's the me who wakes up every day trying to be the best, whether I'm working out or taking my Spanish lesson or enjoying the weekend playing golf. I know we aren't all wired that way. I don't even expect you to be. Everyone learns that different things motivate different people. You don't have to be like me.

You want to be like you. To set goals that you want, that you will get satisfaction from. That will give happiness and purpose to your life. That's how you can go into your retirement fearless and free.

That's what building your future based on the seven core values does for you. It leaves you in a great place ready to take on the world. Life's a journey—enjoy it! Goals can be journeys or they can be destinations. Maybe you want both. Let your money stop owning you, learn to relax, and you can have both.

I'm sure many of you think you are already there. After all, you built that company you now own. Or you spent years crafting that career that made you successful. But I bet you get weekend calls and late-night e-mails and spend more of your vacation doing work than you really want. It's nice to feel needed, but you also need a break.

I want you to imagine being the captain of your own life. Don't let anyone else mutiny and take over. You are in charge. Set aside that cell phone. Walk away from your computer. Put on your captain's hat and smile.

Picture yourself behind the wheel of your very own boat. Maybe you already have a boat. It doesn't matter if it's *Queen Mary*–sized or it's a dinghy. You define the type of boat just as you define the type of retirement you want.

Now you look at the charts and pick where you want to go. Perhaps there's only one major destination, or you might have several stops in mind. Helping others, traveling, going on an archaeological dig, or running a marathon. But you have to have a map to get to that destination.

There's a little island near my house. If I sail to this little island right off the coast and I'm three degrees off course, it's not a problem. I can still see it. I can still get there. The same is true with your money. How can you predict where your money's going to go? Consistent returns keep you from going too far off course.

Now imagine I'm sailing to England from Florida. That's more than 4,000 miles. If I chart a course to England and I'm three degrees off the whole way, I'll never even see it.

The same goes for all of your goals. If you go off course, you will never get to your goal. If you determine you really want to take a cruise to Alaska but spend all your time puttering around the house, you'll only see Alaska on the National Geographic Channel.

You have to set your goals and know how you operate. I knew how to motivate myself when I was running the marathon. I knew how to fight past being sick and sort through all the problems life threw at me.

You might set little goals for yourself to move toward the bigger goal. Like I would tell myself, "Okay, I'm going to run as fast as I can till the next stoplight." Then when I get to the stoplight, I would tell myself that I'd keep the pace up till the next stoplight.

Now it's your turn. It's your turn to try knowing yourself and knowing how to motivate yourself. You have to get inside your own head. What motivates you? What goals matter? What makes you want to run, to travel, to overachieve? What in your wildest dreams makes you happy?

If you're smart and you've picked someone who can help you manage your financial life, you'll have the time and energy for all of that and more.

It's your turn to enjoy life.

DAVE'S TIP NUMBER 7:
Put It All Together

This is more than a book. It's a tool chest. I started off writing about the right skill set you need to either manage your own financial future or find someone else who will manage it for you.

I've been asking you questions all along the way, not to give you the third degree but to help you discover if you have the right stuff to do the job. From years of experience, I can tell you that most people haven't learned how to master the inside game, so they are not likely to live a fearless retirement.

I've known some amazing businesspeople who were forced to recognize that their own skill sets lay elsewhere. You could give them the biggest tool chest in history and some of them still couldn't build a house. The same goes for investing.

The first skill I asked you to focus on is essential—**overprotecting** your money. I asked you how you felt after the last two market collapses. I wanted to know how you handled epic losses to see if you learned anything.

What did you do? Did you go all ostrich and bury your head in the sand, avoiding bad news, whether it was your monthly statements or the evening news? Then, once it all began to sink in, did you rein in your spending and try to dig yourself out? Or did you just keep on doing what Wall Street experts told you?

If that was your strategy, how's it working out for you?

Overprotecting your money isn't just being a tiny bit cautious with your cash. It's taking a foundational approach that ensures you aren't crushed by earthquakes in the market. It throws out some of the accepted Wall Street mumbo jumbo and aims for an approach that fits the investor, not some high-end financial firm.

Next, I followed with questions about **detail orientation**. I can thank my mom for helping put me on the right path here. She was thorough and expected the best out of people—especially me. Every time I catch a mistake—mine or someone else's—I think of my mother and I can see her smile.

So the big question is still an obvious one: Is that who you are? Are you the person who gets irritated at typos and can't stand when things are out of place? Can you be that person every day, or do you lose interest after a time?

If you can't handle details on a daily basis, then you need an advisor to do it for you. Advisors track a mountain of details and have the experience and the tools to do it.

The desire for details and the drive for excellence go hand in hand. I'm sure there are businesspeople and investors who don't focus on details but still manage to succeed. I don't have the statistics, but I bet they are rare.

But success doesn't just happen; it requires **diligence**. Very few people win the lottery and encounter a monumental change in their lives. And when they do, it's usually monumentally bad. Change happens to the rest of us in an incremental way. We wake up a bit earlier; we put in a few more hours of work; we study more and read up to gain expertise; we check and recheck to make sure what we're doing is good and that it works.

It's that diligence, that classic American work ethic, that builds any business. Do you clock in at 9 a.m. and start looking at the clock by 4 p.m.? Or are you in the office early and staying late—even if you aren't compensated for the extra work?

There's a sense of ownership some employees experience when they really become vested in a business. They put in extra hours. They work sometimes on weekends and think about their jobs even in the shower. Then, when they get to the office, they push. They have the drive to succeed and they understand what Thomas Edison is credited as saying: "Genius is one percent inspiration, ninety-nine percent perspiration."[1] That's why one of the ways you can earn part ownership of business is called sweat equity.

Again, I'm not being tough here. I'm asking if you are ready, willing, and able to put in those hours managing your money, or would you rather relax and have a great next thirty years? If you aren't able to put in the time, then you need someone to help you.

Making the hard financial decisions often requires that you possess an adequate level of **coachability** or that you understand the need for a coach, someone to help you learn what you need to know, someone to encourage you to take action when you have to do so. Of course, even professionals need to have some level of coachability to ensure that they are not married to a particular investment model or strategy during changing times.

You need **leadership** qualities to stay on course during tough times. And that's what we've had since 2000, tough and sometimes cataclysmic times. Or you need an advisor with the proper leadership qualities to lead you from the storm to safety. All those skills don't add up to anything if you can't trust your advisor or yourself. Have you been brutally **honest** with yourself about the strengths and weaknesses you bring to the table?

A good team with the right advisor coaching you can fill in those gaps. But if the advisor you are working with doesn't have the track record of honesty, then your advisor can't help you.

The same goes for you. You may be willing to listen and you clearly are willing to learn. But can you honestly say that you are willing to buck Wall Street and protect your money no matter what the "conventional wisdom" says? Because conventional wisdom lets

---

1 Garson O'Toole, "Genius Ratio," *Quote Investigator*, http://quoteinvestigator.com/2012/12/14/genius-ratio/

you ride a market to its top and all the way back down again. Conventional wisdom has given millions of investors headaches and heartaches and resulted in hundreds of billions of dollars in fines.

So be honest with yourself: Can you change? Or are you satisfied with what you've got?

Lastly, it is never too late, whether you want to retire in ten years, this year, or are currently retired. Again, only you know what you want to do. You know that there's a lot more to life than just work—and, believe me, investing is a ton of work. All during your career, you hired experts to grow your business. If you don't trust Wall Street (and you can't) and if you aren't sure you can trust yourself, then your answer is clear. Hire an advisor worthy of all that you've learned. Hire an advisor worthy of you.

It's been a pleasure talking to you. Now turn the page. . . . There's a great offer for you to join our growing group of Americans who call ourselves *The Income Generation*. The party is just getting started and I want you to join us!

EPILOGUE

W HERE AM I going next? Well, on any given Monday through Friday I'm talking to clients in Connecticut or Ft. Lauderdale, shooting my TV show on Newsmax (Sundays, 10 a.m. EST), or working with the advisors who belong to our national network. That network is called Advisors' Academy. I'm very proud of the Academy and even prouder of the financial advisors from all over the country who have joined our organization. Many, like me, are on the major financial TV shows and media outlets like Bloomberg, CNBC, and FOX and Fox Business. They are trusted financial advisors, not salesman—a very important distinction.

We all believe in helping each other; we support our clients and our families based on the seven principles in this book. We believe in our communities and doing right by our clients. Our goal is to help people understand the importance of minimizing their risk and their exposure in the markets, because if a third drop happens—and history tells us it's just a matter of when, not if—then I don't want any one of us born before 1966 to have to suffer the devastating consequences of another downturn or recession.

It's literally why I wrote this book. It's even why I set up my businesses. To help you and to allow you and all my current clients and all the advisors whom I work with around the country to pick exactly what resources will help them the most. Personally, professionally, I really don't care *what* path you choose half as much as I care that you do choose a path. Either way, choose to make your financial situation better. Here's what I have to offer:

- Watch our show, *The Income Generation*, on Newsmax TV each and every Sunday at 10 a.m., EST on the following channels (http://www.newsmaxtv.com/findnewsmaxtv/). We have been so lucky to have guests like Steve Forbes, Mohammed El-Erian, Larry Winget (from the A&E reality show *Big Spender*), and many more. We will continue to do so for you and your loved ones. Recently, we started mixing it up with legends in the sports world. Each week, at the end of the show I offer my audience the opportunity to download a *free white paper* on subjects that they can immediately put into action. They can also call me directly if they have any questions on their financial situation or even if they have suggestions for the show. I make that offer to you too.
- Go to theincomegeneration.com and read our free white papers. On that page you will also find multiple telephone numbers that will help you get in touch with me or my colleagues.
- My registered investment advisory firm (RIA) is called Sound Income Strategies. The principles I espouse in this book are adhered to at Sound Income Strategies. If you go to soundincomestrategies.com, and then click on NEWS, you will see a menu pop up that includes *The Income Generation*. Click on that tab and you will see we have some complimentary educational resources there for you as well. And finally:

Remember, if you are seven to ten years from retirement or if you are already in retirement the first thing you need to do is limit your exposure in the markets and ultimately balance your portfolio for your specific needs. Secondly, decide if you are qualified to manage your money yourself. Or do you need to find the right advisor. Third thing you need to do is take action either way. Because the quality of your life is at stake here. And if you have made it to fifty you already know that you have to build your own happiness. That's right, in the end, just like we were all told by our parents and all those who loved us . . . *it's up to us*—that is, "with a little help from our friends."

David J. Scranton

INDEX